CHRISTIANITY

CHRISTIANITY

Articles from the **IRISH TIMES** *series*

Edited by Patsy McGarry

Published 2001 by
Veritas Publications
7/8 Lower Abbey Street
Dublin 1
Ireland

Email publications@veritas.ie
Website www.veritas.ie

ISBN 1 85390 569 0 (hardback)
ISBN 1 85390 568 2 (paperback)

A catalogue record for this book is available from the British Library.

Veritas books are printed on paper made from the wood pulp of managed forests. For every tree felled, at least one tree is planted, thereby renewing natural resources.

The icon used on the front cover is by Andreas Theodorakis (Rethymnon, Crete). From the collection of Patrick Comerford.

Cover design by Pierce Design
Printed in the Republic of Ireland by Betaprint Ltd, Dublin

CONTENTS

CONTRIBUTORS

Fr Hans Küng is a retired Professor of Dogmatic and Ecumenical Studies at the University of Tübingen, Germany. His publications include *Justification* (1957), *Infallible* (1971), *On Being A Christian* (1974), *Global Responsibility* (1991), *Judaism* (1992), *Christianity* (1995) and *The Catholic Church, A Short History* (2001). In 1979 the Vatican ruled that Fr Küng could no longer be considered a Catholic theologian or function as such.

Professor Michele Dillon is Associate Professor and Book Review Editor of the *Journal for the Scientific Study of Religion* at the Department of Sociology, Yale University. She is the author of *Catholic Identity: Balancing Reason, Faith and Power* (Cambridge University Press, 1999).

Dr Desmond Tutu is the retired Archbishop of Cape Town, South Africa. He won the Nobel Peace Prize in 1984 and in 1995 was chairman of the Truth and Reconciliation Commission set up by President Nelson Mandela. His book *No Future Without Forgiveness*, a personal memoir of the Commission's work, was published in 1999.

Fr Jerome Murphy-O'Connor OP has been living in Jerusalem for the past thirty-eight years where he is regarded as one of the foremost authorities on the historical Jesus. He was also consultant to the recent BBC *Son of God* series.

Dr Racelle R. Weiman is the Director of the Center for Holocaust and Humanity Education at Hebrew Union College, Jewish Institute of Religion. She currently serves on the international steering committee of the Philadelphia-based NGO, Global Dialogue Institute.

Dr Trevor Morrow was elected in 2000 as the youngest ever Moderator of the Presbyterian Church in Ireland, from June 2000 to June 2001. He is a Minister of Lucan, County Dublin.

Rev. Olive Donohoe was a member of the Church of Ireland sub-Committee on Sectarianism. She is rector of the Mountmellick group of parishes in County Laois.

Dr Zaki Badawi is principal of the Muslim College in London and is a regular contributor to debates on Muslim issues in the UK and elsewhere.

Mary Robinson is United Nations High Commissioner for Human Rights. She is a former President of the Republic of Ireland and was previously a Labour Party senator in the Irish Senate.

David Kelso is a former convenor of the Humanist Society of Scotland, and was until recently chief inspector of post-school education at the Scottish executive Education Department. He now works at Glasgow Caledonian University. He writes here in a personal capacity.

Sean Freyne is Professor of Theology at Trinity College Dublin and a Trustee of the Chester Beatty Library. Among his publications dealing with the gospels are *Galilee, Jesus and the Gospels: Literary Approaches and Historical Investigations* (1988) and *Galilee and Gospel: Collected Essays* (2000).

Fr Andrew Greeley is a priest of the Archdiocese of Chicago and teaches at the University of Arizona. He is the author, with Fr Conor Ward, of the report 'How Secularized is the Ireland We Live in?', published in the December 2000 issue of *Doctrine and Life* magazine.

Rev. Patrick Comerford is a Church of Ireland priest and an *Irish Times* journalist. A writer on theology and church history, he is NSM curate of Whitechurch Parish, Dublin.

Patsy McGarry has been Religious Affairs Correspondent for the *Irish Times* since 1997. In 1999 he was awarded the Templeton European Religion Writer of the Year prize by the Conference of European Churches, for his work in 1998.

INTRODUCTION

THE IDEA of this series of essays originated in autumn 1999 when we at the *Irish Times* were considering ways in which the year 2000 might be marked by the newspaper in a particularly Christian way. We felt this should be done as, after all, the entire basis for the second millennium celebrations was the birth of Christ, something that tended to be forgotten in the at times heady excitement generated by the realisation that not only was a century ending but so too was a millennium.

It was also felt that, rather than approaching Christianity in the series from a predictable route, it would be more stimulating to do so through differing and different eyes. So we began with a dissenter, Hans Küng, a man who remains one of the most provocative thinkers in the Christian world today.

Another dissenting voice was that of Michele Dillon, who dealt with Christianity's treatment of women and who articulated a view that is growing ever more vocal and angry, particularly within Catholicism, as women are no longer prepared to accept being treated differently.

One of my own favourite essays in the collection is that by Jerome Murphy-O'Connor on the historical Jesus. Jerry is a big, hearty Corkman whom I met in Jerusalem in March 2000 and whose views on the Jesus of history are fascinating, especially as they are rooted in such depth of research. I attended a lecture he gave at L'École Biblique where he effortlessly held his large audience spellbound. A Dominican priest, he has been in Jerusalem since 1963.

It was in Jerusalem also that I met Racelle Weiman, who I heard speak with refreshing forthrightness about how Christianity had treated Jews over two millennia. Her essay is one of three that look at Christianity from the 'outside'. Dr Zaki Badawi's essay does so from the perspective of Islam, while David Kelso writes from the ever-growing secular/humanist position.

Speaking from the 'inside', in both a Christian and an Irish sense, are Dr Trevor Morrow, Moderator of the Presbyterian Church in Ireland from June 2000 to June 2001, and Rev. Olive Donohoe of the Church of Ireland. Both their essays were published at the time of the North's annual marching season in 2000 and look at the role of Christianity where the Northern Ireland conflict is concerned.

Archbishop Desmond Tutu addresses the issue of conflict resolution from a broader experience, looking at Rwanda, his native South Africa, and Northern Ireland, and advises on the essential requirement of forgiveness for healing in all such places.

Also from a wider perspective, United Nations Human Rights Commissioner Mary Robinson writes about that increasingly complex area of human rights and religion. How one is rooted in the other, and yet how religion can be used to deny those same rights.

Sean Freyne's essay on the origin of the gospels would be in the same historical category as Father Murphy O'Connor's and gives an intriguing insight into the evolution of those documents, which have come to be accepted as telling the story of Jesus and the early church.

In the final essay of the twelve, Father Andrew Greely looks to the future and he finds much hope out there for those who worry about a decline in religion. He reflects on the dismal state of the Christian Church at the end of the first millennium, when its future looked far more bleak, and on recent international findings, which show for instance that nine out of ten Irish people still believe in God.

Part Two of the book is *A Brief History of Christianity* by my colleague Rev. Patrick Comerford. His task was formidable – to write a history of the past two thousand years in twelve instalments with contemporary resonances. I feel he did so terrifically well. Already he has received well-deserved, positive responses. I do not doubt that readers of this book will be just as impressed by his achievement, which should prove invaluable to schools particularly.

In conclusion, I would like to thank the editor of the *Irish Times*, Conor Brady, for being as unequivocal as he was spontaneous in his support for this project when it was first mooted and throughout the year. I would also like to thank Eoin McVey who supplied the finance and Joan Scales who administered it, Joe Joyce who made the page available each month, Sheila Wayman under whose wing it was produced, and Fionnuala Mulcahy who laid it out.

A man who is most deserving of gratitude is my former News Editor Niall Kiely. He was the first person to whom the ideas were mentioned, and his encouragement then made all that has happened them since possible. He and his successor, current News Editor Willy Clingin, were also indulgent where making the necessary time available was concerned. I thank them both.

And of course there's Veritas, and Managing Editor Toner Quinn in particular. It has been a pleasure to deal with such professionals.

Patsy McGarry
June 2001

PART ONE

A DRAMA STILL UNFOLDING

Hans Küng

AT FIRST SIGHT, Christianity today seems very different from the beliefs and practices of Jesus of Nazareth and His first followers two thousand years ago. Roman Catholicism, Eastern Orthodoxy, Anglicanism, the Protestant churches of the Reformation, the liberal Christianity of the modern world, Pentecostalism – now there almost seem to be Christianities, in the plural, rather than a single faith.

If we look back over two millennia to see how this came about, we witness a drama that has unfolded in several acts. Indeed, Christian history is even more complex than that, for none of these acts ends neatly, leading on to the next act. Rather, each of them continues, side by side with its successor, on a stage that becomes increasingly crowded, with many different levels.

Jesus and His first followers were Jews, living in a rural area of a land that, though under Roman occupation, had been shaped by yet another two millennia of history – the history of the people of Israel. Their thinking was stamped by Jewish faith, in one God who had brought His people out of Egypt and given them a promised land, with a king, a temple and a holy city, but who had allowed all these to be taken away by foreign conquerors, inflicting great suffering on them.

Out of this suffering came a new faith, which included the expectation of an end to the present world by God's intervention and the coming of His Messiah. All of these expectations come vividly to life within the pages of the New Testament and stamped the character of earliest, Jewish Christianity.

This earliest Jewish Christianity, however, soon suffered a devastating setback when Jerusalem was again destroyed only forty years after the crucifixion of Jesus. In any case, there was a growing rift between Christians and Jews as, through the work of missionaries like Paul, Christianity spread into the wider Greek world, and into urban as well as rural areas.

Under the influence of Greek philosophy, Christian thinking increasingly adopted Greek concepts and developed great abstract systems, though not without conflicts. 'Heresies' kept splitting the Church, which was constantly in conflict, making it necessary for emperors from Constantine the Great onwards to hold councils intended to keep the peace as well as to define true doctrine. Christianity spread over the East, from Jerusalem, Alexandria and Antioch to Constantinople – later Byzantium – and on to Kiev and Moscow, but in many ways it was a divided Christianity. The complex history of the Hellenistic, Greek and Russian church is an act in the drama that is still continuing.

Alongside it developed another act of the drama, as in the West Rome gained a supremacy over other Churches, and the Pope came to be seen as the head of the true Church, the Roman Catholic Church. During the Middle Ages this Church became a formidable institution, strong enough to take on even the emperor, and wielding immense power, which was demonstrated not least in the Inquisition.

Inevitably corrupted by that power, this Church was clearly in need of reformation. Reform, however, made its mark not within the Church, but through the movement led by Martin Luther in the fifteenth century, followed by Calvin and others, producing the Churches of the Reformation: Lutheran, Calvinist, Methodist, Presbyterian and others.

Another act had begun that is still continuing today. But now, with the eighteenth-century Enlightenment, the modern world was in the making, and all forms of Christianity were under challenge from philosophy and the rising sciences, which posed a threat to the fundamentals of religious belief. The subsequent industrial and technological revolutions represent yet another act in the ongoing drama and one of which we are very conscious today.

This is not yet the end however. The sciences not only posed a threat to religion, but also, especially in the form of archaeology and history, did much to shed new light on the origins and growth of Christianity; indeed it is the sciences that make this portrayal of Christianity possible. And there is a growing awareness that we live, not in a modern but in a post-modern age, in which Christianity may yet, for all its complex and troubled history, find a new place.

It has to be accepted that over this long and complex history there have been many deviations from the original essence of Christianity. There have been gruesome aberrations and signs of decadence, monstrous crimes and blasphemies committed by Christians. One need only recall the persecutions of the Jews and the heresy hunts; the 'holy' wars and the burning of witches, the wars of religion and all the other crimes committed in the name of Christianity.

Despite all the perversions, however, the essence of Christianity keeps breaking through. That raises a question that is difficult to get out of one's head: why has this Christianity kept surviving despite all the un-Christian elements in its history? For like a great river, which has a modest beginning somewhere, and has kept making new cuts through the emergent landscape, Christianity has kept inserting itself into ever-new regions.

In so doing it has experienced violent rejections and undergone revolutions, indeed has itself often caused new shifts in world history. But mustn't we also see here a stream of goodness, mercy, readiness to help, care, which flows from the source, from the gospel, through history? Granted, an infinite amount of debris, flotsam, silt and rubbish has been collected on the long way through the centuries. But has the water at the spring really become polluted, as many people say?

If that is so, how is it that the essence of Christianity did not get lost, but can be recognised time and again – Jesus Christ, His words and actions, His life and death, as an orientation, criterion, model for the concrete life of the individual and the community of faith, for relations with fellow human beings, human society and finally with God?

It is remarkable that time and again, wherever there have not just been words but quite practical discipleship, the spirit of Jesus of Nazareth has managed to establish itself when persons, institutions and constitutions have failed, for the truth of Christianity is not just knowledge of the truth, but existential truth.

So how is it that neither pagan emperors nor 'Christian' dictators, neither power-hungry popes nor dark inquisitors, neither worldly bishops nor fanatical theologians have been able to quench this spirit? Why could the hierarchy never completely veil mutual service of Christians in love, dogmatics never fully veil the discipleship of Christ? What is there about this spirit, that all down the centuries, in an unparalleled movement, it has continually motivated, indeed driven people to break down all the cultural, social, political and religious fortifications, and take seriously the earliest Christian ideal of a love for the neighbour and even the enemy?

It is a strange historical mystery: monks and saints of the early Church appear alongside court theologians and court bishops, Francis of Assisi alongside Innocent III and Boniface VII, Martin Luther alongside Leo X, Catherine of Siena and Teresa of Avila alongside the Grand Inquisitor, Blaise Pascal in the middle of French absolutism, William Booth in the depth of Victorian poverty, Karl Barth, Dietrich Bonhoeffer and Alfred Delp in resistance to the Christianity of a bourgeois culture and National Socialism – not to mention figures in our day like John XXIII, Willem Visser't Hooft, Martin Luther King, Helder Camara and Mother Teresa.

All these known names simply stand as representatives of the countless unknowns whose names are not listed in any church history yet who nevertheless make up the hidden power of Christianity, its true spiritual history. They are representatives of that faith movement consisting of those countless unknowns down the centuries who have gone by the values, criteria and attitudes of the man from Nazareth, who have learned from them that the blessed are those who are poor before God, who do no violence, who hunger and thirst for righteousness, who are merciful, make peace, and will be persecuted for righteousness' sake; who have learned from him to pay heed and to share, to be able to forgive and to repent, to be sparing, practise renunciation and offer help.

To the present day they show that where Christianity really goes by its Christ and allows Him to give it strength, it can offer a spiritual home, a place of faith, hope and love. Time and again they show in the everyday world that supreme values, unconditional norms, deepest motivations and highest ideals can be lived out, indeed that from the depths of belief in Christ suffering and guilt, despair and anxiety can also be overcome.

No, this faith in Christ is no mere otherworldly consolation but a basis for protest and resistance against unjust situations here and now, supported and strengthened by a restless longing for the 'wholly Other'.

Granted, this often hidden history of Christianity is as uninteresting to die-hard critics of Christianity as it is to certain journalists, hot-foot after the sensation of the day. After all, it is much easier to report on a scandal involving a bishop, or a papal visit, than on pastors in the parishes, wearing themselves out in the service of young and old, and still performing this service with a joyful heart and head held high.

But it is precisely these men and women, whether ordained or not, who continue the cause of Jesus Christ. Indeed, there have always been times when little of true Christianity was to be seen in the life and activities of hierarchy and theologians, but when nevertheless those countless, mostly unknown, Christian 'little people' (but always including some bishops, theologians and particularly members of the parish clergy and religious orders) were there to keep alive the spirit of Jesus Christ.

And what kind of a spirit, what kind of a power is it that is at work everywhere? Is everything mere chance, mere fate? No. For believing Christians, beyond doubt there is more involved here. For them it is clear that this effective spirit of Jesus Christ is not an unholy human spirit but the Holy Spirit, the spirit, the power and might of God: God's spiritual presence in the heart of believers and so also in the community of faith.

This spirit sees to it that there is not just research, information and teaching about Christianity, but that

Christianity is experienced with the heart and also really lived out and put into practice – for good or ill, since that is human nature, and in trust in this spirit of God.

So Christians may be sure that Christianity has a future even in the third millennium after Christ; that this community of the spirit and faith has its own kind of 'infallibility'. However, this does not mean that some authorities in particular situations do not make mistakes or perpetrate errors, but rather, that despite all mistakes and errors, sins and vices, the community of believers will be maintained by the Spirit in the truth of Jesus Christ.

In a strange way one feels reminded of the famous advice of the Pharisee Gamaliel, a contemporary of Jesus, who was a Jewish teacher of the law and respected by all the people. At any rate, according to the account in the Acts of the Apostles, after the arrest of the apostles he is said to have remarked to the 'supreme council' in Jerusalem about such Christians: 'If this plan or this undertaking is of men, it will fail; but if it is of God, you will not be able to overthrow them. You might even be found to be opposing God.'

A SECOND-CLASS SEX?

Michele Dillon

AT THE LAST SUPPER, according to scriptural accounts, Jesus broke bread and drank wine with his twelve apostles, all men, and exhorted them to continue this communal practice in remembrance of him. This act is a cornerstone of the Christian tradition and serves as a classic event in the various sacramentalist denominations within Christianity, such as the Catholic, Anglican/Episcopalian, and Lutheran Churches.

The meaning of what occurred at the Last Supper is, however, controversial. To some people it is obvious that, since Christ surrounded himself with only men at the Last Supper, only men can enact the memory of this event – as ordained priests celebrating the Eucharist. To others, it is incidental that it was men who were present. In this view, what is important is not the gender or for that matter the ethnicity (Jewish) or occupation (fishermen) of the apostles but the fact that Christ entrusted his mission to human beings.

Two thousand years later, the significance of the Last Supper is at the centre of the debate (especially within the Catholic Church) over whether women can be ordained priests.

This issue is also part of a broader debate over who has the authority to interpret the Catholic tradition.

More recently, the question of women priests was ignited in the mid-1970s by the decision of the Anglican Church in England to ordain women. The Anglican Archbishop, Donald Coggan of Canterbury, sent a letter to Pope Paul VI in July 1975 informing him of the emerging consensual Anglican view that there were no fundamental objections in principle to the ordination of women priests. The General Synod of the Church of England had passed a resolution to this effect (in June 1975) and had also called for an examination of the theological grounds for including women in the priesthood. The Vatican expressed a contrary view and since then has unequivocally opposed the idea of women priests, despite the theological and historical ambiguities surrounding the question and the fact that a special Vatican-appointed commission concluded it was not possible to settle the issue on the basis of scripture alone.

The Vatican's exclusion of women from ordination contrasts with the prominence of women both in Christ's revelatory actions and during the founding debates of Christianity. The Irish theologian Dermot Lane, for example, offers many illustrations of women's scriptural presence. He observes that women 'are active as witnesses to the resurrection, as deaconesses of the Church, as prophetesses in the Assembly, as catechists in the community and as evangelists of the good news' (*The Furrow*, 1985).

Lane concludes: 'One cannot fail to be impressed by the extraordinary visibility of women in the mission and ministry of Jesus, especially when one bears in mind the predominantly patriarchal culture that existed in first-century Palestine.' He attributes the decline of women's leadership in the Church to a number of societal factors, including the influence of the patriarchal culture of Judaism and Greek philosophy on Christianity, and the early Church's strong opposition to the Gnostic movement in which women were prominent. Dermot Lane concludes that the original vision of Jesus became burdened by social forces that were unprepared 'to accept the unity and equality of all human beings before God and in the service of the Church of Christ.'

Despite the Vatican's upholding of a male-only priesthood, the impetus in favour of women priests is driven by developments within both Church and society. The mid-1970s saw greater economic, political, and social equality for women in Ireland and in Western nations generally, as the barriers hindering women's full participation in society began to be removed.

This new awareness of women's equal status had already been anticipated by Catholic Church leaders who, at the Second Vatican Council (1962–1965), affirmed the equal dignity of women and men. Vatican II also elaborated on the baptismal equality between laity and the ordained, and in *Lumen Gentium*, stated that – as interrelated participants in the one 'priesthood of Christ' – the laity should be given 'every opportunity' to express informed opinions on issues pertaining to 'the good of the Church'.

Vatican II's emancipatory vision of the Church as an inclusive and dialogical community has been realised only partially. The Vatican's continuing opposition to women priests represents, perhaps more than any other contemporary teaching, its commitment to maintaining the male and hierarchical structure of the Church.

The Vatican presents three main reasons for its ban on women's ordination. It argues, first, that to ordain women would contravene the will and intention of Christ who did not call women to be apostles; second, that since women do not physically resemble Christ they cannot mimic the role of Christ in the sacramental consecration of the Eucharist; and third, that a male priesthood is part of the Church's constant and essential hierarchical tradition. In this reasoning, as Pope John Paul II has stated, even if the Vatican wanted to ordain women, it would not be able to do so because of its obligations to maintain what it regards as the institutional blueprint demonstrated by Christ's intentions. The Vatican has thus defined its opposition to women priests as a settled question that is not open to debate and, as recently as 1995, the Congregation for the Doctrine of the Faith declared that this is infallibly taught as part of the 'deposit of faith'.

As many theologians and ordinary Catholics see it, the Vatican's opposition to women priests suggests that women are second-class citizens in the Church. The exclusion of women from the priesthood, simply because they are women, appears to many reasonable people as an injustice in contemporary times, when efforts are being made around the world to give practical recognition to the dignity of all people. Although Church officials do not see the ban on women priests as discriminatory, many Catholic theologians do. The Catholic Theological Society of America (with more than 1,000 members) has raised the possibility that denying women access to the priesthood may in fact be an immoral practice, and as such, is foreign to the 'deposit of faith'.

Equally important, the ban on women priests conveys the impression that the maleness rather than the humanity of Christ is what Church leaders see as essential to Christ's redemptive message. In light of the current shortage of priests, it also suggests that the celebration of the Eucharist, despite its privileged place in the Church's sacramental and communal life, is ultimately less important than ensuring that the Eucharist is not celebrated by a woman priest. On another level, the Vatican's closure of debate on women priests presents a major obstacle to the achievement of greater unity between Catholic and Protestant churches, a goal that John Paul has prioritised in his vision of the Church for this new millennium.

The Vatican's stance on women priests also undermines its own doctrinal emphasis on the fundamental value of women's sexuality. Over the last several years Pope John Paul II has frequently condemned the 'sin of sexism' and the arbitrary ways in which women are discriminated against in society. Although John Paul (in *The Gospel of Life*) advocates the promotion of a 'new feminism' that transforms culture by rejecting 'male' models of domination, his vision of a 'culture of life' excludes the possibility of a Church in which women as priests may embody the life-ethics of Christ.

While the Vatican argues for the complementarity (and equality) of gender role differences, in practice institutional rules that uphold categorical differences – whether with respect to gender or, for example, ethnicity – have been shown to breed invidious comparisons whereby one group is seen as inferior to the other. Independent, therefore, of whether or not the demarcation of gender differences on ordination is intended to be discriminatory, it inevitably is.

It is noteworthy that the majority of Catholics in Ireland, as in Europe and the US, favour women's ordination. Some people who advocate greater equality for women have simply left the Church because they view official Church teaching on the priesthood and issues such as sexuality as hopelessly patriarchal and beyond change. Many who remain involved in the Church, however, actively engage the reasoning offered by the Vatican for its opposition to women priests. In my research with American Catholics I found that the vast majority of those who favour women priests ground their arguments in Catholic doctrine and specifically in the Jesus paradigm.

Whereas official Church arguments defend a male-only priesthood by pointing to the single act of Jesus in choosing only men as apostles, many ordinary Catholics focus on the social rationality of Christ's life as a whole. For them, narrative accounts of Christ's life lead to an alternative theological interpretation that illuminates a pluralistic and inclusive, rather than discriminatory, Jesus. Interviewees typically argued: 'To me, being Catholic means to participate in the Church established by Jesus. Jesus always seemed to espouse the dignity of humankind. To realise that dignity, all people need to be afforded the opportunity to follow their calling, to utilise their individual gifts and talents given to them by their creator. To deny that dignity to half of humankind does not fulfill the example set by Jesus to be Catholic.'

Many Catholics who continue to participate in the Church do so because they have a strong belief in the symbolism of Christ and the possibilities it offers for the Church as a more pluralistic and egalitarian community. As we embark on this new millennium, however, it is not clear whether or how soon we might expect to see women ordained as Catholic priests.

One response to the acute shortage of priests would be to remove the ban on celibacy and allow male priests to marry. This is a relatively straightforward option for the Vatican since it is simply a Church law and thus devoid of the theological complications in which women's ordination is embroiled. It is also the case that people might find it easier to get used to married male priests than to women priests. On the other hand there is evidence, again from the US, that in parishes where women work as pastoral associates – doing the same work as a male priest, except consecrating the Eucharist – they are well accepted, even by those parishioners who tend towards doctrinal conservatism. But even if practical considerations favour married male priests, instead of women priests, this will still leave women's status in the Church ambiguous. It may also signal that the Vatican sees the reclaiming of its interpretive authority as having greater importance than nurturing a communally vibrant Church.

END OF A RECURRING NIGHTMARE

Desmond Tutu

A YEAR AFTER THE GENOCIDE OF 1994 in Rwanda I visited
Ntarama, a village near the capital Kigali, where Tutsis had
been mown down in a church. The new government had not
removed the corpses, so the church was like a mortuary with
bodies lying as they had fallen the year before. The stench was
overpowering. Outside, there was a collection of skulls. Some
still had *pangas* (machetes) and daggers embedded in them. I
tried to pray. Instead I broke down and wept.

The scene was deeply disturbing, and a moving monument
to the viciousness that we as human beings are capable of
unleashing against our fellow creatures. Those who had turned
against one another in this gory fashion had, in many instances,
lived amicably in the same villages. They had spoken the same
language. Many had inter-married. Most espoused the same
faith. Most were Christian.

Their European overlords had sought to maintain their
hegemony by favouring one ethnic group, the Tutsi, over
another, the Hutu. They thus planted the seeds of what would

be one of the bloodiest episodes in modern African history. That genocide also made one pause in blaming racism for every conceivable ill that has befallen humankind. Because while whites had a hand in fomenting the internecine strife in Rwanda, the perpetrators were blacks . . . against fellow blacks.

A few kilometres from the church in Ntarama, women had begun to build a settlement, which they named the Nelson Mandela Village. It was to be a home for widows and orphans created by the genocide. The women said: 'We must mourn and weep for the dead. But life must also go on; we can't go on weeping.' Wonderfully impressive. Indomitable.

At Ntarama, you might say, there was Calvary, death and crucifixion. In the Nelson Mandela Village there was resurrection, new life, new beginning, new hope. It was noteworthy, again, how women have this remarkable resilience and instinct for nurturing life.

I visited the overcrowded prison at Kigali. It was packed to the rafters with people suspected of being involved in the genocide. Almost all were Hutu. There were men and women. Even young children. People of every age and from every social group – including priests, nuns, teachers and lawyers. Some had died from suffocation. I told the country's President, Pasteur Bizimungu, that the prison was a disaster waiting to happen and that it would add to bitter memories and exacerbate the resentment of the Hutu towards the Tutsi.

At a rally in the main stadium at Kigali I said the story of Rwanda was a typical history of 'top dog' and 'underdog'. Top dog wanted to cling to a privileged position. The underdog strove to topple top dog. When that happened the new top dog engaged in an orgy of retribution to pay back the new underdog for all the pain and suffering inflicted when it was top dog. New underdog fought like an enraged bull to topple new top dog. It stored in its memory all the pain and suffering it was now enduring, forgetting that new top dog was – in its view – just retaliating for what it remembered suffering when new underdog was master. A sad history of reprisal provoking counter-reprisal.

I reminded the Tutsi that they had waited for thirty years to get their own back for what they perceived to be the injustices that had been heaped on them. I told them extremists among the Hutu were also capable of waiting thirty years – or more – for the day when they could topple the new government. Then, in their turn, they would unleash devastation, revenge and resentment. I discussed the talk about tribunals. People did not want to tolerate allowing the (mainly Hutu) criminals escape punishment. What I feared was retributive justice. If it was to be the last word in their situation, then Rwanda had had it.

There is no way that most Hutu were going to be persuaded that the courts would find them guilty because the evidence is incontrovertible, or that any court, anywhere in the world, confronted with such evidence, would pronounce them guilty. They would feel they had been found guilty, not because they were guilty, but because they were Hutu. And they would wait for the day when they would be able to take revenge. Then they would pay back the Tutsi for the horrendous prison conditions in which they were then being held. I told the Tutsi that the cycle of reprisal and counter-reprisal that characterised their national history had to be broken, and that the only way to do this was to go beyond retributive justice to restorative justice; they had to move on to forgiveness, because without it there was no future.

The president of Rwanda responded with considerable magnanimity. They were ready to forgive, he said, but even Jesus had declared that the devil could not be forgiven. I do not know where he found the basis for that, but he was expressing a view that found a resonance. There were atrocities that were unforgivable. But I was given a fair and indeed friendly hearing. Why was I not rebuffed? Why did these traumatised people, who had undergone such a terrible experience, listen to an unpopular point of view? They listened because something had happened in South Africa. It gave them reason to pause, and wonder.

The world had expected that a ghastly bloodbath would overwhelm South Africa. It did not happen. Then the world thought that, after a democratically elected government was put in place, those who for so long had been denied their rights, whose dignity had been trodden underfoot, callously and without compunction, would go on the rampage, unleashing an orgy of revenge and retribution that would devastate their common motherland. Instead, there was the remarkable Truth and Reconciliation Commission. Before it people told their heart-rending stories. Victims expressed a willingness to forgive. Perpetrators told stories of sordid atrocities, and asked the forgiveness of those they had wronged so grievously.

The world could not believe what it was seeing. South Africans managed an extraordinary, reasonably peaceful transition from the awfulness of repression to the relative stability of democracy. They confounded everyone by their novel manner of dealing with a horrendous past. That is what enabled me to address my sisters and brothers in Rwanda in a manner that under other circumstances might have been seen as insensitive and presumptuous.

I have had the same experience in other parts of the world where people are seeking to face their history. In 1998 I was in Dublin and Belfast. In both cities audiences warmed to the lesson of our South African experience – that there is hardly any situation which could be said to be devoid of hope. Our problem was one which many had believed was intractable. I told them in Dublin and Belfast that 'Yes, we have lived through a ghastly nightmare, but it has ended.' They, too, were on the way to an end of their nightmare, I said. For had there not been the Good Friday Agreement?

I told them they ought not to become despondent at obstacles preventing the implementation of that crucial agreement. Our experience in South Africa had been that, frequently, the enemies of peace responded to breakthroughs by redoubling their efforts to derail the process. I told them to redouble their own determination and vigilance to ensure that such a priceless gift as the end of their 'Troubles' would not elude them just when it was within their grasp. I told them that in South Africa it had often felt as if we were on a roller-coaster. At one moment we experienced the most wonderful joy, euphoria even, at some new and crucial initiative. We would see the promised land of peace and justice round the corner. Then, just when we thought we were on the last lap, something ghastly would happen. A massacre, a deadlock, brinkmanship of some kind, a walk-out by one delegation or another. And we would scrape the rock bottom of despair and despondency. I told them this was normal. As sure as our nightmare had ended so would theirs. As sure as night followed day.

I visited the Holy Land over Christmas 1989 and had the privilege of going to the Holocaust museum in Jerusalem. When I was asked for my impressions afterwards I said it was a shattering experience. But I added that the Lord, whom I served and who was Himself a Jew, would have asked, 'But what about forgiveness?' It set the cat among the pigeons.

I was roundly condemned. I had also expressed dismay at the treatment meted out to Palestinians. I was charged with being anti-Semitic. Graffiti appeared on the walls of St George's Anglican cathedral in Jerusalem. It read 'Tutu is a black Nazi pig'. So I was apprehensive about going back to Jerusalem again in January of last year. I need not have worried. My hosts in Jerusalem had to turn people away. It was clear everywhere that what occurred in South Africa fascinated people greatly. There was deep interest among Israelis in the process of the Truth and Reconciliation Commission, and in the concept of forgiveness and reconciliation. In South Africa we also happened to be blessed with leaders who were ready to take risks. When you embark on the business of asking for and giving forgiveness, you are taking a risk. If you ask another person for forgiveness you may be spurned. Or the one you have injured may refuse to forgive you.

The risk is greater if you are the injured party, wanting to offer forgiveness. The culprit may be arrogant, obdurate or blind; not ready or willing to apologise or to ask for forgiveness in their turn. He or she thus cannot receive the forgiveness they are offered. Such rejection can jeopardise the whole enterprise. Our leaders were ready to say they were willing to walk the path of confession, forgiveness, and reconciliation, with all the hazards that lay along the way. It seems their gamble is paying off. Our land has not been overwhelmed by the catastrophe that once seemed so inevitable.

It is crucial when a relationship has been damaged, or when a potential relationship has been made impossible, that the perpetrator should acknowledge the truth and be ready and willing to apologise. It is never easy. In almost every language the most difficult words are 'I am sorry'. So it is not at all surprising that those accused of horrendous deeds, and the communities they come from – for whom they believed they were committing those atrocities – almost always try to find ways out of admitting that they were capable of such deeds. They adopt the denial mode. When the evidence is incontrovertible, they take refuge in feigned ignorance. The Germans claimed they did not know what the Nazis were up to. White South Africans also tried to find refuge in claims of ignorance. But Leon Wessels, the former apartheid cabinet minister, was closer to the mark when he said that they had not wanted to know.

Forgiving and being reconciled are not about pretending that things are other than they are. It is not a patting of one another on the back or a turning of a blind eye to the wrong. True reconciliation exposes the awfulness, the abuse, the pain, the degradation – the truth. It may even make things worse. But in the end it is worthwhile. Because in the end there is real healing from having dealt with a real situation. Spurious reconciliation brings about only spurious healing. And in forgiving people we are not being asked to forget. On the contrary. It is important to remember, so that we will not let such atrocities happen again. Nor does forgiveness mean condoning what has happened. It means taking what has happened seriously and not minimising it. It is a drawing out of the sting of memory that threatens to poison our entire existence. Without that there really is no future.

DESTINY'S CHILD

JEROME MURPHY-O'CONNOR

MARY LIVED IN BETHLEHEM as the second wife of Joseph, who had six children – four boys and two girls – by his first wife. Understandably the small one-room house in the north-west corner of the town was rather crowded. It was no place for a woman to give birth. The men certainly would not inconvenience themselves for the sake of a mere woman. It was up to Mary, assisted by her female relatives, to find a quiet place. They went out to the nearby cave that the family used for stabling and storage. There she gave birth to Jesus and laid him in the manger.

At this time, probably about 5 or 6 BC, Bethlehem lived in terror. After a savagely oppressive rule of thirty years, the king, Herod the Great, was dying. As his grip weakened, long repressed hostility to him began to make itself felt. In response, Herod's secret police kept a very close eye on Bethlehem, because the prophet Micah had predicted that it would be the birthplace of 'a ruler who will govern my people Israel'. The inhabitants knew that Herod, who had executed three of his own sons, would wipe out their town completely if the thought entered his diseased mind.

Joseph was luckier than other Bethlehemites. His skill as a carpenter gave him mobility. To play it safe, he decided to take his family to Egypt until Herod was out of the way. When news of the king's death arrived, they planned to return to their home. Then they heard that his successor in Judea was the hated Archelaus, who had good reason to feel insecure. The danger to Bethlehem had increased rather than diminished. It was no time to go back there. Then Joseph had a stroke of luck. Antipas, another son of Herod the Great, inherited Galilee.

Antipas came into a territory ruined by war. His capital, Sepphoris, had been flattened by the Romans in 3 BC when they put down the rebellion that followed the death of Herod the Great. Antipas' first concern was to rebuild, and the word went out that he was recruiting labour. Joseph, with many others, responded. Too shrewd to put his family in the midst of a great work-camp with many single men, Joseph lodged them in the nearby village of Nazareth. The hour's walk to work in Sepphoris was a small price to pay for their security, and he could build up a business there against the day when work on Sepphoris finished.

Jesus grew up in Nazareth. His language was Aramaic. At school, which was obligatory from the age of five to thirteen, he would have learned enough Hebrew to read the Scriptures. The great work-camp at Sepphoris would have been a magnet for little boys. There he would have picked up a smattering of Greek, which was everyone's second language.

Mary told Jesus that God had chosen him for a special destiny, but that was all she could tell him. When she and Joseph brought him to Jerusalem for Passover at the age of twelve, he used the opportunity to question the teachers in the temple as to what God wanted of him, but got no satisfaction.

Jesus had to wait for nearly twenty years until a prophet appeared. He was a relative, John the Baptist, who was preaching on the east bank of the Jordan across from Jericho. In the hope that John could interpret God's will for him, Jesus made the four-day journey from Galilee to be baptised.

In that moment Jesus' life changed. He abandoned his trade and became a disciple of the Baptist. He rose to become John's second-in-command. Thus when John decided to carry his message to the more densely populated area west of the Jordan, he entrusted Judea to Jesus, while he himself took the much more difficult task of preaching to the Samaritans who detested the Jews.

Not surprisingly, Jesus was much more successful. Eventually John decided to cut his losses in Samaria, and moved to Galilee, the only other Jewish area he had not reached. There his commitment to the law of Moses obliged him to criticise the marriage of king Antipas to Herodias, the wife of his half-brother Philip.

For the sake of this new union, Antipas had had to repudiate his Nabataean wife. Her father, Aretas IV of Petra, moved troops to his northern frontier to avenge the insult to his daughter. To meet them, Antipas garrisoned the great fortress of Machaerus just east of the Dead Sea. He could not leave John the Baptist to criticise him in Galilee. So he arrested him and brought him with him to Machaerus. As soon as Jesus got word of the imprisonment of John, he left Judea and went north to replace him in Galilee. Jesus was now the leader of the Baptist movement and had to move into what proved to be a position of great danger. He lodged in Peter's house in Capernaum.

In Galilee, Jesus at first proclaimed John's message of repentance, symbolised by baptism. Unsurprisingly, Antipas and the crowds thought of him as a second John the Baptist, and for a time his life was in peril. Antipas, however, soon lost interest, because Jesus' ministry evolved in a completely different direction to that of John the Baptist. While he worked with John, Jesus demanded obedience to the law of Moses. After John's arrest, Jesus became a friend of tax collectors and 'sinners'. 'Sinner' here has a technical meaning. It designates a person who practises one of the despised trades. These were occupations notorious for leading to dishonesty.

Tax collecting was a prime example, but anyone in the transport business (donkey or camel drivers, sailors) could easily pilfer, and herdsmen could sell wool or meat on the sly. By eating with such as these, Jesus publicly accepted them as they were. He did not ask them to change. He had recognised that they were not vicious but victims. They were forced into one of the despised trades by failing to find other employment.

Jesus' offer of table-fellowship proclaimed that 'sinners' were not what the law said they were. This had enormous consequences. By disobeying one commandment, Jesus effectively rejected the whole law. He committed himself to a position diametrically opposed to what John and he had once insisted on.

In a word, he repudiated what he had thought to be his vocation. He realised that he was not called to be a prophet. From this point on, the standard characteristics of Jesus' ministry emerge clearly. Firstly, he proclaimed his superiority to the Jewish law both in word and in deed. He said things like: 'You have heard that it was said [in the law] . . . but I say to you [something much more important].' He also ignored the prohibition of work on the Sabbath. This amounted to an implicit claim to be the Messiah. For Jesus, this insight into his destiny was reinforced by the realisation that he had the power to work miracles. He cured the sick and raised the dead. Would such powers be given to one who falsely claimed to be the Messiah?

No longer did Jesus' preaching demand obedience to the law. Instead he proclaimed the kingdom of God. He bade his disciples to pray to the Father that God would one day come to rule as king. The advent of God's kingdom would mean the abolition of poverty, hunger and sorrow. Gentiles would share the eternal banquet with the Israelite patriarchs. In addition, Jesus maintained that this kingdom was in some way already present in his ministry. God's merciful power was here and now in the healings and exorcisms of Jesus, and in his whole-hearted acceptance of outcasts.

The radical change in Jesus' message and comportment deeply disturbed John the Baptist in prison. He sent messengers to ask Jesus what was going on. In response Jesus said, 'Go and tell John what you see and hear: the blind see again, the lame walk, lepers are cleansed, the deaf hear, the dead are raised, and the poor have the good news preached to them. And blessed is he who takes no offence at me.' (Matt 11:4-6) The concluding beatitude is a delicate invitation to Jesus' old teacher to abandon his vision of the day of the Lord as one of darkness and punishment, and to recognise the beneficent hand of God in what Jesus was saying and doing.

Despite Jesus' conviction that he was God's chosen Messiah, he had to struggle for fidelity. He had to contend with the pull of a family that did not believe in him. He had to struggle against the fear of physical injury leading to death. He had to resist the seduction of wealth and power. He had to pray for light in situations where God appeared to be demanding contradictory things of him.

The initial enthusiastic response to Jesus in Galilee soon waned. He made few converts, and even his closest followers did not always completely understand. He decided to transfer his ministry to Jerusalem. If he was successful there, there might be a trickle-down effect in Galilee.

When Jesus was in the Jerusalem area, he lodged with Martha, Mary and Lazarus in the village of Bethany on the eastern slope of the Mount of Olives. Each morning he walked over the hill to preach in the temple, and returned in the evening. He was not well received. Hostility gave way to threats of violence. Jesus was forced to flee to Peraea, the other side of the Jordan, but he returned at the request of the sisters to raise Lazarus from the dead. For the High Priest, Caiaphas, that was the last straw, and a warrant went out for Jesus' arrest. He went into hiding again, this time in Ephraim, a village on the fringe of the Judean desert.

Aware that time was running out, Jesus arranged for a last meal in Jerusalem with his disciples, during the course of which he instituted the Eucharist. On his way back to Bethany that night, the sight of the great moon-lit tombs in the Kidron valley made him aware that his death might be very close. A tremendous internal struggle for self-mastery took place in a place called Gethsemane. By the time Jesus had recovered, it was too late to continue his journey. Judas had arrived with temple police who arrested him. A kitchen cabinet hastily convened by the High Priest found Jesus guilty of blasphemy. The Jews, however, could not condemn him to death. That was a prerogative of the Romans. Thus Caiaphas transmuted Jesus' proclamation of the kingdom of God into a denial of the authority of the Roman emperor, and presented the case to the Roman governor, Pontius Pilate.

Reluctantly, Pilate had Jesus scourged and condemned him to the atrocious penalty of crucifixion. On Friday April 7th, AD 30, the duty centurion led Jesus through the crowded streets with the crossbeam tied to his outstretched arms. The end of that terrible journey was an abandoned quarry just outside the north wall of Jerusalem. The vertical beam had been set up on a little promontory in the eastern cliff that had eroded to the shape of a skull. Jesus' hands were nailed to the crossbeam, which was then dropped into place. His feet were nailed to the upright. He hung there in agony for some six hours before dying.

After permission had been given by Pilate, some of Jesus' disciples took down the body. In the far side of the quarry an entrepreneur had cut a catacomb. The body of Jesus was laid in the first empty chamber, and the entrance was closed by a stone to preserve the body from jackals and wild dogs. Two days later the women disciples of Jesus found the tomb empty.

ENDING THE BITTERNESS

RACELLE R. WEIMAN

I FEEL DEEPLY FORTUNATE and grateful to be alive in the twenty-first century. You see, I am a Jew. My people and faith have been scattered, persecuted, subjugated and murdered. We have been falsely accused of the most horrendous, despicable acts and been labelled sub-human, nonhuman, Christ-killers and satanic. We were forcibly separated, and also separated ourselves, from our persecutors and accusers. We knew little about their world and they knew less about ours, though we occupied the same spaces and breathed from the same cultural and social environments.

What meaning does this have for Christians reflecting on the new millennium? Everything, according to historians, sociologists, ethicists, and theologians of both traditions. The Jewish historical experience of anti-Semitism has been the direct result of the Christian Churches' discomfort, confusion and outright supressionist relationship to Judaism and the Jewish people. So why might a Christian be interested and even rejoice in my survival? Because the Christians and Jews are moving toward rapprochement and understanding at the dawn of this new century.

It is good news for the Jews, but it is therapeutic and invigorating for Christianity. Liberating itself from hatred and prejudice, and armed with a new appreciation for God's pluralistic love, Christians are recognising that 'God does not repent of the gifts He makes, or of the calls He issues' (Romans, cited in Vatican II), and can begin courageously to face their own responsibility toward history with repentance and healing. Though Pope John Paul II insisted he was making a personal pilgrimage when he visited Israel this spring, it was clear that he was finalising the process of reconciliation between the Catholic Church and the Jewish people that began with the *Nostra Aetate* declaration at the Second Vatican Council in 1965. The image of the Pope praying at the Western Wall of the Holy Temple, the most precious site to Judaism, is the picture most cherished and remembered by the people of Israel.

The Vatican's recognition of the state of Israel in 1993, coupled with the Pope's visit this year, puts to rest ugly ghosts of the past, such as the myth of the wandering Jew and exclusion from grace as divine punishment. The Jewish people can begin to trust the Church that has condemned anti-Semitism, confirmed God's continued covenant with the Jewish people, and renounced Christian mission to the Jews. The dissonance between church and synagogue has probably led to one of the longest and definitely the most painful of conflicts in the history of the world. The negation of Jewish existence translated into political and social terms. Christianity, celebrating two thousand years of continued resilience, must come to a sobering and reflective moment when it necessarily remembers its prominent role in setting the stage for the Holocaust. This silence was deafening.

So loud was the silence of the Christian Churches during the Holocaust – the extermination of one-third of all the world's Jews in the epicentre of Christian Europe – that it stunned all those who stopped to listen. And amid that silence a frightening sound was heard: the rumbling chorus of whispers and rumours and murmuring that came out of the church pews and books and seminaries and gave assent to and empowered the civilised barbarians of Nazism.

It was with horror that Christians in the last half of the twentieth century realised that for nearly two thousand years they had been encouraging what Fr John Pawlikowski of the Catholic Theological Seminary in Chicago called 'bad theology'. The turning point for many Christians came after they were exposed to the rigorous scholarly work of French historian Jules Isaac, who, while mourning the murder of his wife and daughter among the ashes, asked: 'How Auschwitz?' His answer was in the seminal work of 1948 called *Jesus et Israel,* or *The Teaching of Contempt,* which documented the systematic anti-Semitism propagated by Christianity through the centuries.

It reached Pope John XXIII. As a result, the gentle Pope wrote a small prayer, which had enormous consequences: 'We see the sign of Cain written in our faith. For centuries our brother, Abel, has been lying in his blood shed by us. Forgive us the curse we uttered against the name of the Jew. Forgive us, that in their flesh, we crucified You again.'

One of his first acts as Pope in 1959 was the elimination of sinister passages about 'perfidious Jews' from the Catholic liturgy for Good Friday. His greatest achievement was his convocation of the Second Vatican Council, whose original purpose was to expel anti-Judaism through a clear and unambiguous declaration. John XXIII died in 1963 before he saw his dream realised, but under Pope Paul VI, 2,222 bishops approved a Latin statement condemning anti-Semitism and the deicide charge against the Jews. They reminded their flocks of the Jewishness of Jesus and the early Church, and that the Church today 'draws sustenance from the root of that well-cultivated olive tree onto which have been grafted the wild shoots, the Gentiles' (Rom 2:17). It became a challenge of reform and change to its own churches and seminaries, and set off the chain reaction of similar or even finer statements from Protestant Churches worldwide.

Numerous scholars point out that all the Churches – Catholic, Protestant and Orthodox – agree on one issue alone: that the proclamation of the Gospel accompanied a refutation of Judaism. For many centuries the Jews were pushed to the margins of Christian society. The fifteenth-century humanist, Erasmus of Rotterdam, said: 'If it is Christian to hate the Jews, then we are all good Christians.'

By the Middle Ages, the Jews experienced every form of humiliation: in addition to being forced to wear distinguishing badges by Pope Innocent III's Fourth Lateran Council; ghettos were erected; books were burned; discriminatory laws and heavy taxes levied; expulsions and pogroms decreed; and pornographic art and vicious lies were circulated about the Jews.

Fr Edward Flannery demonstrated, in a comparison of canonical laws and Nazi measures, that anti-Judaism had been a prominent part of Christian society. The Church administrations had provided the Nazis with a blueprint for almost all their actions, with the exception of the technologically advanced death factories. What is often overlooked is that Jesus, mother Mary, Peter, Paul and the disciples would all have been sent to those very same crematoriums.

Courageous Christians who told the truth about the animosity and hatred were often ostracised or ignored. Even before the second World War, Anglican scholar James Parkes' doctorate at Oxford began a search called 'The Conflict Between Church and Synagogue'. In horror at his findings of the deep-seated Christian animosity and competitiveness, he devoted his life to uncovering anti-Judaism within the early Church, which shaped Christian thought.

The Scottish Catholic Church historian Malcolm Hay published in 1950 a searing indictment called *Thy Brother's Blood*. He wrote to Jules Isaac that 'Auschwitz would have been impossible had not it been for the poisonous lies, which the Churches have infected Christian populations with for at least 1600 years'. Though publishers initially refused to publish it, Hay's book eventually played a considerable role in framing the Vatican II statement.

Theologians such as the American Protestant A. Roy Eckardt understood the issues relating to a sibling-like conflict in his Elder and Younger Brothers. The younger and newer faith community, Christianity, coming from within and as an outgrowth of a rich and developed older faith tradition, Judaism, was desperately trying to attract the attention of the parent God. The attempted negation of the Jews is built directly upon issues of birthright and jealousy, which produces the uneasy claim of being chosen. Scholars discovered that combating covenants and competing testaments were the theme of preaching by early Church fathers by the fourth century. Additionally, the persecution and crushing defeat of the Jewish Revolt of AD 66–70 caused the Gospel writers to shift the Christian alliance to Rome, and thus to present the Jews as the enemy. It was also an era that read events such as military defeats as acts of God illustrating His displeasure.

The paradox in the retelling of the passion is that a story of a Jew (Jesus) who was put to death by the Romans tragically was retold as if he was a Christian put to death by Jews! The initial reason for the arrest of Jesus – which was for suspected political subversion against the Roman government ('King of the Jews' affixed above his 'crown') – became an accusation of blasphemy. This created an illusion that there was a rift between Jesus and his own Jewish people.

The sociologist and Benedictine monk Vincent Martin studied the common roots and parting of the ways between synagogue and church while he was in Jerusalem at the Hebrew University. His work is an example of the happy new reality of Christians coming to the Land of Israel, interacting and studying with a living and vibrant Jewish community. He, and many modern Christians from all over the world, is learning the Hebrew language and reading the experience of Jesus and the early Church in Jewish historical context, with local archaeology and Jewish scriptural resources assisting. This kind of experience is two-sided as many Jews are enriched through the exposure and interaction with such academics as the Dominican Fr Marcel Dubois, who was chair of the Philosophy Department at the Hebrew University for decades.

Together, Jews and Christians can study each other's traditions and share in commemorations such as Holocaust Memorial services and the Passover Seder. We can engage in interfaith dialogue, religious education initiatives, charity and social justice issues worldwide. We will find areas of disagreement and deep chasms between us, and we will find areas where religious faith and ethical uprightness will demonstrate that we are the closest of allies in an increasingly secular and Godless world.

The Jews were an endangered species, ending the twentieth century with much fewer numbers than when that sad and violent century began. They have been resurrected through the return to their eternal homeland, the revival of the spoken modern Hebrew language and the gathering of their dispersed communities from all the continents of the world.

As a result of the lessons of the Holocaust, the world saw fit to create the Universal Declaration of Human Rights and the Genocide Convention in 1948, the same year that the state of Israel was reborn. It is crucial to consider that the last thirty-five years of the twentieth century brought a remarkable and, hopefully, permanent rethinking as regards the Jews, in the documents of the Churches, in the writing of the liturgy and theology, in the revision of textbooks and the teachings of the catechisms. All of this, as well as the stress on religious dialogue, were the result of Vatican II's *Nostra Aetate*, which may have been the most important outcome of the flames of the Holocaust.

Together, Jews and Christians of integrity must monitor the unfolding of such events as the new presentation of the Oberammergau Passion Play 2000, the canonisation of certain popes and individuals, and Church statements on the Holocaust, with an understandably critical eye. The concern for righteousness and compassion and the end of triumphalism and displacement are our obligations for the new millennium. Our ongoing dialogue can serve as a beacon of hope for reconciliation in other conflicts, and create a living model for peace for both the secular and the faithful.

In 1948, Albert Camus illustrated how the eyes of all look toward religion for guidance and the moral imperative: 'For a long time [during the Holocaust] I waited for a great voice to speak up in Rome. I, an unbeliever? Precisely, for I knew that the spirit would be lost if it did not utter a cry of condemnation when faced with force . . . millions of men like me did not hear it and believers and unbelievers alike shared a solitude . . . Christians should speak out, loud and clear and they should voice their condemnation in such a way that never a doubt, never the slightest doubt, could rise in the heart of the simplest man . . . [Christianity must] confront the blood-stained face of history.'

AN ISLAND OF PEACE

TREVOR MORROW

PAUL BRADY FROM STRABANE, one of my favourite singers and songwriters, could have written *The Island* in Galilee in the first century. Remember those haunting lines: 'Up here we sacrifice our children to the worn-out dreams of yesterday'. In Jesus' time, the people around Tiberius had experienced major atrocities that reinforced their sense of corporate identity and moral outrage. All the elements with which we are familiar were present. Galilee, you see, was the heartland of ethnic nationalism. And, whether our brand is Irish or British we can identify with it. The Romans had ultimate authority, but it was the Herodians, those at the court of Herod Antipas, who controlled the region on their behalf.

The Zealots – paramilitaries – represented those who believed that a just solution could be achieved through guerrilla warfare. Their arsenals were probably hidden in bunkers around Capernaum. The Pharisees saw themselves as the true custodians of Jewish traditions. They were honoured and revered. They had maintained the sacred traditions of their fathers.

There had always been a strong religious dimension to this nationalism, but secularism was also a phenomenon. Listen to Rabbi Yohanan ben Zakkai, who declared in his frustration at the time, 'Galilee, Galilee, you hate the Torah'. Nevertheless, deep within the psyche of the Jew, whether secular or religious, was the hope that one day Shalom, peace, would come. The Messiah would appear and destroy the enemies of the people. So the wicked would be punished and the righteous would be vindicated. Justice would be established. It is into this painful cauldron of ethnic nationalism, religious piety and cynical secularism that Jesus comes. It is to Mark, the gospel writer, that I want to turn to show you what happens.

What strikes us immediately is that the ministry and message of Jesus were so shocking and radical that within the first few chapters of Mark's account Jesus provokes an unholy alliance between the religious and political establishment: 'Then the Pharisees went out and began to plot with the Herodians how they might kill Jesus. They hated each other but now they hated Jesus even more.' (Mk 3:6)

The gospel can only be heard in the twenty-first century if we realise that we in Ireland, North and South, have got it entirely wrong. Here on this island, our expectations, our agenda, the paradigm within which we think and act, the attitudes and fears and prejudices that we have imbibed with our mother's milk, in fact all of those things that have fed and nourished an ethnic and political tribalism, of these we must repent if we are to believe and live and share in the good news of the kingdom.

Let us remember that Mark, the gospel writer, is not primarily a storyteller or a reporter. He's a teacher. He is self-consciously selecting material, almost certainly from the eye-witness accounts of the apostle Peter, in order that we might understand who Jesus is and what he is about. It is at this point that Mark deliberately establishes the heart of Jesus' message over and against the prevailing view of the religious establishment, specifically that of the Pharisees.

The Pharisees have had a bad press. They had a noble history from the second century BC as people who had preserved with honour the traditions of their fathers. They had a genuine concern for what was 'right', both in terms of the keeping of the law and in opposition to such practices as a social class system. They had among them men of integrity like Nicodemus and Joseph of Arimithea. But, at the heart of their thinking and behaviour was a religion based on law. When you did what was right (according to the law) God rewarded you. When you did what was wrong he punished you. It's still a popular theology, even today. Their assumption was that the more they sought to keep the law the more righteous they were and the more God would hear their prayers. Specifically, he would fulfil their messianic dreams and would bring peace to their land. Sounds familiar?

The clear implications were that their political and national aspirations were dependent upon the keeping of the law. That is, if they did what was right they would receive what they deserved. Their enemies too would get what they deserved. They would be defeated and a new day would dawn. In comparison and contrast, and that's how Mark tells it, the message of Jesus is totally different. Instead it is a declaration of complete forgiveness. What he offers is not for those who have kept the law but for those who have broken the law. It is not for those who are in the right but for those who are in the wrong. It is not something we have merited it is something that we do not deserve.

That is why we have at this point in Mark's Gospel the story of the paralytic. This poor man is brought by his friends and, because they cannot enter the house, a hole is made in the roof and he is lowered to the feet of Jesus. When Jesus says to him 'your sins are forgiven you' the teachers of the law, the Pharisees, are appalled. For them this is blasphemy. Only God can forgive sins. Of course, they are right. But to reinforce what is at the heart of Jesus' ministry, he asks them, 'What is easier to say, "your sins are forgiven you or get up and walk."' Of course it was easier to say 'your sins are forgiven'. Nobody can see what is going on inside our hearts. So therefore, says Jesus (and this is the key verse of this entire section), in order that you might know that the Son of Man has authority on earth to forgive sins, 'Stand up, take up your mat and walk.' And immediately he gets up, grabs his bed, and walks off.

Here Jesus establishes clear water between his ministry and that of the establishment. Jesus above all else is in the business of forgiveness. This is central to his life and mission. For the simple reason that this is our greatest need. It is our greatest personal need and it is our greatest social need. This is not because we are suffering from what Freud described as a pathological condition of guilt. It is because we are all morally responsible. And all of us have failed.

In forgiveness, the one who is offended embraces the pain that the guilty deserves. And then he offers a total pardon from our past, an opportunity to wipe the slate clean, and to start all over again. This is the Jesus way for Shalom, for peace. It is in total contrast to those who want only the wicked to suffer and the righteous to be rewarded. Having focused on the priority of forgiveness as central to his ministry, Jesus now proceeds to do something even more outrageous to the establishment, he creates a community of the forgiven and the forgiving.

For the good Jew there are two types of people: the righteous – those who sought to keep the law – and the sinners. Sinners referred to those who were unacceptable; they had neither the education, the time, nor the inclination to keep the law. They were the 'am-haaritz', the ordinary people of the land. So when Jesus wants to create a community of the forgiven who does he go to? That's right, a tax collector, Levi. Jesus says to him 'follow me' and immediately he drops everything and follows him. Being a rich man he decides to celebrate this with his friends, other tax collectors and sinners who have also received forgiveness and have come to follow Jesus. In his home, the first Presbyterian Church in Capernaum, a gathering of radical dissenters is formed.

They have a marvellous party with Jesus as their chief guest. As you can imagine, the Pharisees are appalled. This is just plain wrong. The *Mishnah*, the encyclopaedia of Pharisaeic legalism, is quite specific. 'A Pharisee may not be the guest of one of the people of the am-haaritz', the people of the land. So they ask the question: How can a man of God eat and drink with tax collectors and sinners? Jesus' response is 'those who are well do not need a physician'. He says, I have not come to call the 'righteous' but 'sinners'.

Here then is the sign of how things ought to be. Jesus begins to establish this new community from the alienated and lost in society. He does not begin with the nice people, but with the tax collectors and prostitutes and paramilitaries and then moves to Samaritans and Roman centurions. He invites women as well as men. He brings in the slaves and the free. And he invites his followers to make disciples of all nations, from all the wrong sort of people. Is it any wonder that in Galilee, this small but potent, radical new society was such a threat to the religious and political establishment and 'the Pharisees began to plot with the Herodians to kill him'?

Let me address my fellow Presbyterians for whom I have some responsibility in leadership during this year. In the light of God's word, I want us to rediscover our role and calling on this island at this time in two areas. Firstly, if we were to ask most people what we stand for, they may not answer in exactly such terms, but what they would mean is that what we believe in is 'the law'. The impression is that we are against so many things. We are opposed to this and unhappy about that. It is an image of negativity. The irony of all this is that the Reformation was about the rediscovery of something positive and joyful – that salvation was *sola grati* (grace alone). In other words, that our total and complete forgiveness, the pardon of all our sins, was not for the deserving but for the undeserving.

No community, including our own, is immune from suffering or wrong-doing. But, because we have received mercy, now is the time for us to reach out our hand to those who have caused us pain and to offer forgiveness. Secondly, we need to rediscover what it means to be radical dissenters, that is, part of the Church catholic but not part of the establishment. From the sixteenth century we have been a movement for reformation and renewal. We have been thrawn, awkward and difficult at times. In our history we have defied prelates, priests and popes. On occasions, we have defended monarchs or encouraged rebellion. But, the one controlling factor in all of this was that we would not accept any other ultimate authority except Jesus himself.

In these momentous days in the history of Ireland, we have an opportunity to see emerging congregations, Presbyterian churches, that are different from the tribal allegiances of the past. Women and men who are Celts and Anglo-Saxons, republicans and unionists, those who feel comfortable speaking Irish, or Ulster Scots or English, hurlers and cricketers, IT consultants and welders, held together not by cultural identity or political aspiration but, as in that little church in Capernaum, only that they are followers of Jesus.

They have been forgiven and are forgiving. Such communities will represent on this island the true radical dissenting tradition and without a doubt, as in our Presbyterian past, they will be extremely unsettling to the political and religious establishment.

All of this might seem unrealistic and, in the light of Irish history, impossible. Where 'we have tried to carve tomorrow from a tombstone'. But our situation is, in essence, no worse than Galilee in the first century. It is the same Jesus who can change things. He is here.

As Christians, we in Ireland in the twenty-first century have an apparently impossible task. We have, as neighbours and friends, ordinary people who are paralysed by sectarianism or are in bondage to secular materialism or, to use the language of the apostle Paul, are just spiritually dead. There are days when we just seem to be enveloped in oppressive, hopeless darkness. The greatest need of this hour is for Irish women and men to hear again the powerful liberating word of Christ: for listening to his voice new life the dead receive.

If we are a reformed church, *ecclesia reformata, semper reformanda,* i.e. reformed and always reforming, then as we plan strategically for this new millennium there ought to be no political traditions that we will not question, no cultural customs that we will not challenge, no sacred cows that we will not sacrifice, so that this generation will not only see Jesus but hear the faith empowering word of God.

NO LONGER BOUND BY OLD TIES

Olive Donohoe

A REPORT TO THE CHURCH OF IRELAND General Synod in 1999 stated that it has become a matter of deep shame that an act of worship should be followed by displays of hostility, hatred and lawlessness. It was referring to events at Drumcree. The feelings expressed then have, if anything, been deepened within the Church of Ireland by events at Drumcree and beyond in recent years.

The report, by the Church's sub-committee on sectarianism, stated that it would be disingenuous to pretend that the events, the emotion, and indignation engendered by successive confrontations at Drumcree and along the Garvaghy Road in Portadown, reported so widely in the media, did not set a context and provide motivation for the setting up of this sub-committee. Their brief was to undertake an examination of Church life at all levels, to identify ways in which the Church may have been deemed to be accommodating to sectarianism . . . and as a means of combating sectarianism, promoting at all levels of Church life tolerance, dialogue, co-operation and mutual respect between the Churches. Not to do so is to promote sectarianism.

And the report acknowledges that there is little doubt that in the eyes of many the 'Drumcree crisis' is a microcosm of the sectarian agonies of Northern Ireland and it is especially distressing that a parish of the Church of Ireland and its church building should appear at the very heart of that agony.

The report in its entirety is set into context with the section 'Theological Reflections on Sectarianism'. Here, the theological and biblical imperative is expressed; first of all, that God is love, and secondly, that this love is revealed most profoundly in Jesus Christ. These two tenets would appear to be radically at variance with any manifestation of sectarianism – where God is open, sectarianism rejects.

The point is made that while it is important to recognise that the Church of Ireland shares associations with the Orange Order spanning a period of more than two hundred years, and that although many members of the order are also members of the Church of Ireland, the Church has moved from some of the positions that, in the past, the two may have shared. It is therefore fair to say that in certain respects the Church of Ireland and the Orange Order have parted company, and that the Church has failed to draw this parting of the ways to the attention of the Orange Order.

The sub-committee took great pains to examine and to attempt to describe the relationship between the Church of Ireland and the Orange Order. It also sought to pull together an objective analysis of what the order claims to stand for and whether these claims fit in with the position of the Church of Ireland at the beginning of the twenty-first century. In considering that relationship, the sub-committee defined its task as not to evaluate the various loyal orders in their own right, but rather to identify ways in which the Church of

Ireland may be deemed to be accommodating to sectarianism
in those organisations, if and where sectarianism exists, and
whether the sectarian practices of those organisations impinge
on the life of the Church.

The report states that by facilitating the attendance of the
Orange lodges of the Portadown District at the church service,
the Church of Ireland is perceived by many to be
accommodating, to a degree, the violence that occurred
subsequently; it is argued that if the parade from the church
service had not taken place, then there might not have been the
circumstances for civil disorder.

It also states that there are no formal links between the
Church of Ireland and the Orange Order. There are, however,
many informal links that have been established since 1795, and
today there are three main points of informal contact. These
are that some members of the Church, clerical as well as lay, are
members of the order; some Church of Ireland services are
attended by members of the order; and some Orange halls
were used by the Church of Ireland for Church purposes.

Recognising that the Church of Ireland may be deemed to
be accommodating to sectarianism by association with certain
aspects of the order's teaching and practice, the sub-committee
identified clear differences between the Church and the Orange
Order. First of all, the report recognised that the Orange Order
is a religious society with many high ideals, but that in its
requirements for membership it adopts an anti-Roman Catholic
stance. The report acknowledges that these views have now
been superseded by a spirit of mutual respect and the
acceptance of denominational integrity. In addition, in a section
titled 'Drumcree', the sub-committee said the Church of
Ireland could be seen as accommodating to sectarianism by
association with certain aspects of Orange Order conduct at
Drumcree. The Church responds to this suggestion by

identifying clear differences between itself and the order at Drumcree.

Because of the presence of the Orange Order at the parish church in Drumcree it is often thought that the Church of Ireland supports the range of issues surrounding the annual Orange Order parade to the church on the Sunday before July 12th. The reality is quite different. The report goes on to state that it is a matter of deep regret that the Church of Ireland should have been in any way identified with the civil disturbances and confessed that, under the circumstances, regret was insufficient and must be combined with remedial action.

The commitment of the C of I is to promote tolerance, co-operation and mutual respect between the Churches and society. Not to do so is to promote sectarianism. It has become a matter of deep shame that an act of worship should be followed by displays of hostility, hatred and lawlessness. It also stated that for all its international notoriety the situation at Drumcree is infinitely complex.

With regard to inter-Church relations, it is often thought that the Church of Ireland identifies with the Orange Order's outlook on relations between the Churches today. Again, the reality is quite different. The Church of Ireland is fully engaged in inter-Church relations with the Roman Catholic Church, both in Ireland and worldwide. The Church's official record demonstrates that for many decades it has been at the forefront of ecumenical endeavour. As to the Orange Order's claim to be composed of Protestants, united and resolved to the utmost of their power to support and defend their religion, the report pointed out that there was as yet no single body of doctrine uniting all those Churches and groups calling themselves Protestant.

The Church of Ireland, it noted, is strongly supportive of

efforts to promote the visible unity of the Church. It also gives itself the responsibility of defining, defending and interpreting – in the light of Holy Scripture – the faith it has received. On the place of Holy Scripture, the report states that much of scripture, as represented by the various loyal orders, including the Orange Order, is of the Old Testament, with an emphasis on such things as battle, righteousness, the defeat of evil, and obedience to the law.

While affirming the centrality of Holy Scripture in all of life, it submitted that, in the loyal orders, insufficient emphasis is ostensibly given to the New Testament, in particular to those teachings of Jesus Christ who manifested in his earthly ministry – and in his redeeming work on the cross – God's love for all people, and who called us to the love of God and our neighbour, to love our enemies, and who gave us the golden rule, to treat others as we ourselves would wish to be treated.

Recognising the changes in the Church of Ireland, the report emphasised that since the sixteenth century the Church, like most Christian Churches, has changed. It has gained new insights. It recognised that in the Church's history on this island we, as the established Church, had been party to conquest, oppression and discrimination against our fellow Irish people – members of other Churches. It also acknowledged that its history and that of the Orange Order were intertwined.

While differences between the Churches had often been handled in a confrontational manner up to the mid-twentieth century today, in the Church of Ireland, differences with our fellow Christian Churches are handled through dialogue, recognising that the common faith that we share is more than our differences.

The report goes on to say that changes were further evidenced in the inter-Church activities of the Church of Ireland, and many of those in the forefront of work for reform and justice in society have been members of the Church. In the twentieth century much encouraging change took place in breaking down the centuries-old barriers between the Churches, it added.

The Church's commitment to, and involvement in, the ecumenical movement went back to the Edinburgh International Missionary Conference of 1910. In 1968 the Church was instrumental in setting up the Ballymascanlon Conference, while in the 1970s it initiated the custom of inviting observers from other Churches, including the Roman Catholic Church, to its General Synod every year. With regard to attitudes to the law, the report pointed out that while the Orange Order did not recognise the lawful determination of the Parades Commission, the Church of Ireland supported the lawful exercise of civil power and has taught respect for the law. It noted also that many members of the security forces – army and police – have been, and are, members of the Church.

Therefore, it was of great concern to the Church to observe scenes of lawlessness and violence at Drumcree and elsewhere. These deplorable acts of aggression create an atmosphere of heightened tension in which atrocities such as the murders of the Quinn children in Ballymoney and, as a result of the violence deriving from Drumcree, the death of a policeman, have taken place.

As a further indication of the differences between the Church of Ireland and the Orange Order, the report said the Church respects the State and its authority. Historically, and by contrast, the Orange Order has had a conditional relationship with the State. It added that the order has accepted the authority of the State, in so far as the succession of the throne remains Protestant. The report goes on to say that the order also had a party political as well as a religious agenda. It states that the Church has no party political allegiance and included and welcomed into its membership people of all political persuasions, and none.

Finally, the report, quoting from the Order's own *Qualifications of an Orangeman,* noted that the order exhorts its members 'to an humble and steadfast faith in Jesus Christ . . . and to cultivate truth, justice, brotherly kindness and charity'. It also noted the Order's explicit commitment to tolerance of difference, quoting that it 'will not admit into the Brotherhood persons whom an intolerant spirit leads to persecute, injure or upbraid any man on account of his religious opinions.'

The sub-committee was at pains not to be seen as demonising the loyal orders – to do so would be to act towards them in a sectarian fashion, it said. It commended an attitude of constructive engagement, encouraging the orders to move as the Church has moved.

The section of the report dealing with the relationship between the Church and the loyal orders concluded:

> We believe that in order to show itself a truly Christian movement it is now time for the Orange Order to show that the love of God, love of neighbour and obedience to the New Testament principles take priority over mere party advancement.
>
> We believe that exclusivity is contrary to the teaching and example of Jesus Christ and that inclusivity, therefore, must be the hallmark of our Christian actions.

The sub-committee stated that it offered its comments in charity so as to inform not only the members of its own Church (who may or may not be members of the Orange Order), but also the Order itself and the wider community, which has a right to be reminded of such divergences.

A TIME FOR EAST
AND WEST TO JOIN FORCES

ZAKI BADAWI

CHRISTIANITY AND ISLAM, together with Judaism, spring from the same Abrahamic roots. The religion of Abraham upholds the principle of monotheism and the belief in a personal deity. Islam is distinguished from Christianity by its rigorous monotheism and an inclination towards transcendentalism, while it differs from Judaism by its universalism.

The doctrinal differences between Christianity and Islam, though important, cannot possibly justify hostility between them. Indeed the Holy Qur'an says of Christians 'Thou [Mohammad] wilt find that, of all people, they who say, "Behold, we are Christians", come closest to feeling affection for those who believe [in this divine writ]: this is so because there are priests and monks among them, and because these are not given to arrogance.' (Sura 5:82). And also: 'And thereupon We caused [others of] Our apostles to follow in their footsteps; and [in the course of time] We caused them to be followed by Jesus, son of Mary, upon whom We bestowed the Gospel; and in the hearts of those who [truly] follow him We engendered compassion and mercy' (Sura 57:27).

Islam believes in the virgin birth and the ascension of Jesus Christ to heaven. It venerates the Virgin Mary in a manner indistinguishable from that of many Christians. Those Christians may find it surprising how close Christianity is to Islam. Indeed, a Muslim who does not accept the message of Jesus and who fails to venerate the Virgin Mary would be regarded as an apostate.

If the two religions are so close in basic beliefs, they are closer still in their cultural heritage. Both of them adopted the Hellenistic culture, which they adapted to their monotheistic beliefs and enriched with the depth of their contribution. Throughout the Middle Ages the universities and scholars of Muslim Spain were the leaders in all areas of intellectual, scientific, and technological endeavour. The Arabic language was, for almost a thousand years, the lingua franca of the cultural elite of the world.

Sharing a religious ancestry and a cultural source should have made the two faiths allies, not enemies. Regrettably, Islam and Christianity have historically met more often on the battle fields than in the debating chambers. Their conflicts were often described as religious wars. The most celebrated of these conflicts were the Crusades in Palestine and Spain, which to this day colour Muslim perception of Christians and the West. Indeed, in today's reporting of Western activities in the Muslim world they are always described as the new Crusades.

I have always maintained that 'religious wars' are a contradiction in terms. The essence of religion, and especially the Abrahamic religions, is peace. Life, and especially human life, is sacred. All of them have inherited this from the experience of Abraham when he proceeded to sacrifice his son and found a ram in his place, sent by God as a lesson to humanity that the Lord of the Universe shuns human sacrifice.

When a religion descends to shedding blood in its own cause it betrays its principles and becomes idolatry. Wars are embarked upon for territorial aggrandisement, control of resources and dominance over others. Religion is wheeled in by politicians, generals, and colonists, to dignify their base ambitions and to mobilise the pious innocent.

In today's world, the need for going back to the basis of our faith has become an urgent necessity. Not only is this essential for our common good and mutual understanding, but for the very survival of our two faiths. Religion is now faced with the most serious challenge in its history. The phenomenal development of science has reduced the area human beings used to consider to be the province of God alone. In the past, God was perceived as the cause of the phenomena that human beings could not comprehend. But the expansion of our knowledge of the world has given us such self-confidence that many scientists have expelled God from their laboratories and banned faith and ethics from their scientific thinking.

Many scientists believe God resides in the dark corners of human ignorance and that He abandons them at the first glimmer of scientific light. The victories of science have given a fillip to the secularist movement. Many a secularist now argues that religion in every shape or form is a collection of irrelevant myths that prey on the human intellect and enslave humanity to backward ideas and hidebound morality. Clearly this challenge is so serious that it should engage our full attention and divert us away from conflicts among ourselves.

We cannot deny the achievements of science. We are powerless to stop or even limit the impact of technology. But a technological and scientific world needs a faith to give a meaning to the material world and a purpose to the life of a human being. Christianity and Islam, standing shoulder to shoulder rather than face to face, can save humanity from Godless despair and anarchical morality. The break-up of families, the disintegration of communities, the growth of individualism and materialism, may have been the inevitable consequence of substituting secular science for religious faith.

Humanity needs religion and ethics as well as science and technology. This, however, demands new interpretations of the religious texts to take note of the scientific discoveries. This should not be an invitation to theologians to read science and scientific theories into the sacred texts. It is simply an invitation to purge our theological work of outdated concepts about the physical world.

To move forward in this way requires a number of things. First, the two faiths must come to grips with each other's fundamental beliefs. There should be no room for misunderstanding or misrepresentation. Our common monotheism is interpreted differently by both faiths. Let us understand the differences and move forward in the battle against secularism and atheism.

Second, the two faiths share common ethical values, based on the principles of justice and social welfare. We should together proclaim these principles to the world. We must invite world leaders to close the widening gap between rich and poor. We must alert the more advanced countries to the needs of the less advanced in literacy, health, and employment opportunities.

Third, our two faiths must encourage all societies to live up to the principles of good government. A government that excludes its people from participation and stands above accountability should be rejected by our faiths as being tyrannical and devoid of any ethical or religious legitimacy.

Fourth, our two faiths must inject moral values into the media, which has become so powerful that no other force appears to be capable of restraining it, and so influential that it has become the guide that decrees the rules of conduct. It has arrogated to itself the power to undermine all institutions, especially the religious institutions, while claiming for itself to be beyond reproach. It has often exploited a single misdemeanour to tarnish the reputations of an entire profession or faith. We should co-operate together to inject ethical restraints into the media to make it more an instrument of good and less a threat to our values and our society.

Fifth, our two faiths should seek to rescue humanity from its preoccupations with rights and alert everyone to the principle of duty. Our two faiths are duty-oriented rather than rights-oriented. Human rights are sanctioned in both our faiths as duties to God. The right to live can be based on the principle of 'Thou shalt not kill'. The other commandments can be seen as sources for the other rights listed in the Universal Declaration of Human Rights.

Religion, and especially the Abrahamic religions, are often labelled male-dominated religions. Women seem to be given an inferior position in the religious scheme of things, be it in the place of worship, the family, or society. We need to stand together and recover the principle of equality enshrined in our two faiths. The Qur'an often repeats and emphasises the high status of women. The Arabs at the time of the Prophet (*pbuh*) denied their womenfolk the freedom to choose their husbands or to free themselves from an unhappy marriage. They also denied them the right to own property or to participate in public life, and female infanticide was widespread. Islam revolutionised the position of the woman and granted her equality in the teeth of well-entrenched, hostile custom. Admittedly, not many Muslim societies live up to the high standard enshrined in the Holy Qur'an and the Prophet's Tradition, but together we can help each other to find our pristine principles and adhere to them.

Sixth, we both should support the principle of tolerance, which should go beyond the mere negative acceptance of the other. We should be committed to each other, caring for each other's needs and securing for each other the protection and support due to people of the same family of faith. This is particularly urgent where the adherents of one religious faith live as a minority among the majority of the other faith. Islam has always recognised Christians as the People of the Book and accorded them autonomy in belief and social customs. The example of Spain at the zenith of its civilisation remains to this day a beacon to the world in providing an environment for different religious faiths to dialogue with each other in unity and open mindedness.

There are, of course, obstacles to the programme suggested. There is history. Muslims still remember the atrocities committed by the Crusades in Palestine and the draconian rule of Ferdinand and Isabella of Spain. On the other hand, Christians still subconsciously hear the war drums of the Turkish armies at the gates of Vienna. For all the weakness of the present-day Muslim world, many in the Christian world still consider it to be a mortal danger. Though it is difficult to unburden ourselves of the unhappy legacies of the past, we must exert our energy to look to the future rather than backward into history.

The second obstacle is the present-day conflict of interests. The Western world, which is seen by us (Muslims) as primarily Christian, has in modern times imposed its will on all Muslim nations, plundering their resources, deciding their destiny, violating their laws and traditions and sometimes imposing upon them unpopular rulers. We should together stand against this injustice and call upon our co-religionists to seek the common good of all.

The third obstacle is the stance of the Christian world against the Palestinians in the calamity that has befallen them. Their plight, which is authored by the Christian world, appears not to trouble the Christian conscience. This is regarded by the world of Islam as a complete negation of moral and religious principles. We should together stand to see that the Palestinians are treated as human beings and not as a cumbersome problem to be disposed of in the manner of the genocide practices of the past.

The fourth obstacle is the sense of superiority from which we both suffer. The Christian world claims cultural superiority and heaps contempt on the current situation in the Muslim world, whereas we Muslims proclaim our religious superiority and question the monotheistic commitment of the Christians. Perhaps the two of us can look at the positive aspects of each other and move forward in dignity and mutual respect.

For all these obstacles I feel optimistic about the future co-operation between Islam and Christianity. The advocates of the theory of inevitable conflict between the two cultures ignore the fundamental similarities between both faiths. They harp on the dynamic of historical events to drag us into conflict. Strangely, the adherents of this theory of inevitable war between our two faiths are the extremists on the side of the Muslims who legitimise war not only against non-Muslims but also against other Muslims. On the side of the Christians are those who, enticed by the Huntington theory of the conflict of civilisations, exaggerate skirmishes in Nigeria or Indonesia or the Balkans as evidence of the correctness of that theory.

Both groups miss the point. The vast majority of Muslims and Christians are peace-loving and aspire to create a world inspired by the love of humanity as a manifestation of the love of God.

HUMAN RIGHTS AND RELIGION

MARY ROBINSON

SHORTLY BEFORE the world's Heads of State and Government met in New York for the United Nations's Millennnium Summit, a less publicised but no less important meeting took place in the same city. For the first time, one thousand religious and spiritual leaders gathered for what was called the Millennium World Peace Summit. They came from all of the great faiths, including Bahai, Buddhism, Christianity, Confucianism, Hinduism, Indigenous Peoples, Islam, Jainism, Judaism, Shinto, Sikhism, Taoism and Zoroastrianism. The goal of the Religious Summit was to identify ways that the worldwide religious and spiritual communities can work together as interfaith allies with the United Nations on specific peace, poverty and environmental issues.

I welcomed the holding of the Religious Summit for many reasons, and was encouraged by its outcome. It was highly appropriate because of Article 18 of the Universal Declaration of Human Rights and the Declaration on the Elimination of all forms of Intolerance Based on Religion or Belief, adopted by the UN General Assembly in 1981, which I discuss below.

Religious leaders have great power to strengthen respect for human dignity. Their active support and involvement are essential if the goal of universal human rights is to be achieved. I believe that there should be a more intense dialogue between religious leaders and the human rights community. We have a great deal in common – perhaps more than is sometimes realised.

But, in everyday life, how many of us take the time to speak to or learn from people with different faiths or backgrounds? An experience that I found enlightening was when my office organised a seminar with Islamic scholars to discuss Islamic perspectives on the Universal Declaration on Human Rights. What was interesting was that, in all the discussions, no one expressed doubt about the relevance of international human rights standards. Rather, there was emphasis on accepting international standards, including the Universal Declaration, in promoting and protecting human rights at the national level. Attention was drawn to how human rights are actually lived. The principles of Islam relating to human dignity and social solidarity are a rich resource from which to face the human rights challenges of today. Islamic concern with human dignity is old; it goes back to the very beginning. The message I took from the Islamic seminar was the importance of dialogue between different cultures and religions. We must get away from the tendency to be deaf to, and even to demonise, cultures and religions different from our own.

There can be no denying that religion is often a pretext used to justify violation of human rights. It is heartening, therefore, that the outcome of the Religious Summit took the form of a commitment on the part of the religious leaders to work closely with the UN 'to promote the inner and outer conditions that foster peace and the non-violent management and resolution of conflict.'

The final statement of the Religious Summit says much about the relationship between religion and human rights. It speaks of the UN and the religions of the world having a common concern for human dignity, justice and peace; it says that religions have contributed to the peace of the world, but have also been used to create division and fuel hostilities; it notes that in an interdependent world, peace requires agreement on fundamental ethical values; and it concludes that there can be no real peace until all groups and communities acknowledge the cultural and religious diversity of the human family in a spirit of mutual respect and understanding.

It is important to emphasise the common ground between religion and human rights – and between religions themselves – because difference is often accentuated, usually to justify assaults on the rights of others. The best description of the relationship that I have come across was spelt out by Vaclav Havel and is worth repeating:

> I am convinced that the deepest roots of that which we now call human rights lie somewhat beyond us, and above us; somewhere deeper than the world of human covenants – in a realm that I would, for simplicity's sake, describe as metaphysical. Although they may fail to realise this, human beings – the only creatures who are fully aware of their own being and of their mortality, and who perceive their surroundings as a world and have an inner relationship to that world – derive their dignity, as well as their responsibility, from the world as a whole; that is, from that in which they see the world's central theme, its back- bone, its order, its direction, its essence, its soul-name it as you will. Christians put it simply: man is here in the image of God.
>
> The world has markedly changed in the past fifty years. There are many more of us on this planet now; the colonial

system has fallen apart; the bi-polar division is gone; globalisation is advancing at a dizzying pace. The Euro-American culture that largely moulded the character of our present civilisation is no longer the predominant. We are entering the era of multi-culturalism. While the world is now enveloped by one single global civilisation, this civilisation is based on coexistence of many cultures, religions or spheres of civilisation that are equal and equally powerful.

Havel was speaking two years ago on the occastion of the fiftieth anniversary of the Universal Declaration of Human Rights, that great post-war enunciation of the fundamental rights to which everyone is entitled, simply by virtue of being human.

The accusation is sometimes made that the Universal Declaration is a Western-engineered document; even that it is an attempt to be a substitute for religion – 'a doctrine for those who believe in nothing else', as one commentator put it. The records of the drafting of the Universal Declaration show that this was far from being the intention. The drafters sought to reflect in their work the differing cultural and religious traditions in the world. Representatives of African, Asian, and Latin American countries played a prominent role in the drafting, the results of which were intended to be a distillation of major legal, religious and philosophical beliefs.

As the Preamble puts it, the thirty Articles of the Univeral Declaration are 'a common standard of achievement for all peoples and nations.' The Universal Declaration and the covenants and conventions that it inspired spell out the individual's fundamental rights and show how these can be achieved and protected. The essence of human rights is that they are universal: they apply to everyone, wherever they live. The right to freedom of conscience and religion is a central tenet of the Universal Declaration of Human Rights. Article 18 states:

> Everyone has the right to freedom of thought, conscience and religion; this includes freedom to change his religion or belief, and freedom, either alone or in his community with others and in public or private, to manifest his religion or belief in teaching, practice, worship and observance.

These rights are elaborated in the Declaration on the Elimination of all Forms of Intolerance Based on Religion of Belief adopted by the UN General Assembly in 1981. As well as expressing the conviction that freedom of religion and belief could contribute to peace and social justice, the Declaration calls on States to take all effective measures to prevent and eliminate discrimination and appropriate measures to combat intolerance on the grounds of religion or belief.

Sadly, there is no shortage of examples of assaults on freedom of conscience and religion in many parts of the world. The UN Commission on Human Rights felt it necessary to appoint a Special Rapporteur on Religious Intolerance to examine incidents and governmental actions inconsistent with the 1981 Declaration and to recommend remedial measures.

Among the global trends identified by the Special Rapporteur are: (i) a tendency to perpetuate policies, legislation and practices that violate the right to freedom of religion or belief; (ii) the spread of religious extremism; and (iii) persistent discrimination and acts of intolerance affecting vulnerable groups such as minorities and women.

The Special Rapporteur, whose title is to be changed to the Special Rapporteur on Freedom of Religion and Belief, plays a useful role in alerting the international community to his findings. However, the cases highlighted tend to be individual instances of intolerance and discrimination rather that the root causes.

Attention has been drawn to the need for elaborating preventive strategies and for promoting dialogue between the religions. In this regards, the words of Theo Van Boven, in his seminal work *Religious Freedom in an International Perspective: Existing and Future Standards* are worth quoting:

> What is at stake in the promotion and protection of religious liberty is not the search for objective truth but the enhancement of respect for the subjective rights of individuals or groups of individuals and communities. On the basis of this understanding, the measures of implementation, at a national and international level, should focus on the promotion of constructive dialogue between religious communities themselves and between these communities and the public authorities in a spirit of tolerance and respect.

I am glad that Ireland has been active in the efforts to promote the right of freedom of conscience and religion by acting as sponsor for the annual Resolution on this topic at the Commission on Human Rights and through support for the work of the Special Rapporteur on Freedom of Religion and Belief.

The international community struck a blow against discrimination on the grounds of religion or belief at the World Conference against Racism, which took place in South Africa from August 31st to September 7th, 2001.

The full title of the Conference included not only racism and racial discrimination but also xenophobia and related intolerance. Since religious difference is so often used as a pretext for categorising individuals or groups of people as different, I believe that the World Conference can play an important role in devising new measures to fight this scourge.

That is why, when I circulated a Visionary Declaration against Racism reasserting the value of tolerance and diversity on the occasion of the Millennium Summit, I made sure to bring this initiative to the attention of the religious and spiritual leaders who gathered in New York and to ask for their endorsement.

The Visionary Declaration was launched by President Thabo Mbeki of South Africa and is placed under the patronage of Mr Nelson Mandela. More than fifty leaders have signed, including the Taoiseach, and many others are planning to sign in the near future.

The Visionary Declaration recognises that racism, racial discrimination, xenophobia and related intolerance persist because they are rooted in fear: fear of what is different, fear of the other, fear of the loss of personal security. It says that we are all members of one human family and that, instead of allowing diversity of race and culture to become a limiting factor in human exchange and development, we must re-focus our understanding, discern in such diversity the potential for mutual enrichment, and realise that it is the interchange between great traditions of human spirituality that offers the best prospect for the persistence of the human spirit itself. I see the Visionary Declaration as serving to promote tolerance and diversity as a vision for the twenty-first century.

The World Conference was the ideal occasion for governments to adopt a declaration and a detailed, practical plan of action which will provide the standards, the structures, the remedies – in essence, the culture – to ensure full recognition of the dignity and equality of all, and full respect for human rights. I look forward to the valuable support of all the world's religious and spiritual leaders in this most worthwhile cause.

FAITH AND REASON
ARE CONVERGING

DAVID KELSO

ONE OF THE CHARMS – and perversities – of the English language is that it can be ferociously precise in such matters as the difference between *continuous* and *continual* or the nuances of meaning among *ease*, *leisure* and *idleness*, yet basic concepts such as equity and religion remain undefined. *Humanism* is another such word.

As a young Catholic growing up in the west of Scotland, I first met the word in contexts inhabited by similar monsters such as *communism* and *anarchy*. Clearly humanism was a bad thing. Imagine my confusion then when I learned that the thinking that underpinned the Renaissance (a good thing) was also described as humanism. Were these two totally different uses of the same word, or had the context changed so fundamentally that what was good in 1560 was bad in 1960 – like burning heretics?

Sure enough, it is in the nature of abstract ideas that their meanings evolve. *Democracy* in the eighteenth century had connotations of mob rule and domination of the best by the many (perish the thought), while for Demosthenes it didn't involve very many people at all.

Music once had something to do with the Muses, while *sophistication* wasn't very different from casuistry. That is why *humanism* can mean such different things to different people. A value-system derived from the human perspective may be perceived as base compared with the transcendental perspective, or magnificent against the backdrop of a million years of human development. As the man said: 'Things look different from different places.'

To many readers that idea may seem trite, even self-evident, yet the implications for our cherished belief systems are enormous. If ideas such as democracy, equity, justice and truth have evolved over the past two thousand years or more, might the same not be true of religion, divinity, the spiritual, morality – and humanism? And, if so, how reliable are all the esoteric distinctions we have been busily creating and refining for the past four hundred years or so, and for which so many people have died? I should like to propose that many of these dichotomies are in fact obsolete and unhelpful.

I arrived at this view by a lengthy and at times painful journey from Catholicism through secular humanism to where I am today. Humanism is in many ways a natural alternative for those disillusioned with Catholicism. Revelation is replaced by reason; absolute authority by pluralism and tolerance; superstitious tradition by progressive scepticism; and divine grace by human rights.

That is why humanist values and perspectives are now so prevalent in advanced societies, even within the traditional religions. Its one major shortcoming, I discovered through personal experience, is an underestimation of the importance of the non-rational (as distinct from *irrational*), the affective, the *spiritual* in human experience. No doubt because the origins of modern humanism lie in a rationalist revolt against the authoritarian anti-rationalism of mainstream Biblical Christianity, the emphasis in humanism remains on a responsible, rational (albeit humane) approach to the problems of human life.

This makes for good social policy, sane economics and an admirable approach to world development, but is less immediately relevant to the private world of grief, loneliness, fear and doubt. It is no accident that the mainstream religions, with some five thousand years of experience behind them, have developed elaborate and comprehensive approaches to these aspects of life: ritual, prayer, reflection, confession and so forth.

While my early personal experience was of mutual hostility and incomprehension between the forces of faith and reason, I was to discover twenty years later that this need not be the case. There are *religions* that feel no need for dogma and authority, and can, thus, very successfully combine the strengths of rationalism with sensitivity to people's spiritual needs. Probably the best known is Buddhism, which insists on no unchanging doctrines but only that each individual must search within her/himself for truth, understanding and ethical direction.

A similarly non-dogmatic approach is to be found in branches of Hinduism and in the Chinese Taoist tradition. Closer to home, I was to discover that throughout the history of Christianity there has been a persistent anti-authoritarian tradition, represented today by the Society of Friends (Quakers) and the Unitarians (in the US Unitarian-Universalists), both of whom are content to accept their rich Christian (indeed, Judaeo-Christian) pedigree, building on it to seek the truth wherever reason and reflection lead.

There is even a strand of *religious humanism*, well developed in the US, but more apparent on this side of the Atlantic as a variant of other traditions than as a distinct approach in its own right. And, of course, all of the major churches have a large, and growing, liberal wing, which is more often than not recognisably humanist (or at least rationalist/naturalistic) in character.

Could it be, I wonder, that there is no substantial theological, philosophical or ideological dichotomy between the rational and the scriptural; the naturalistic and the transcendental; the secular and the sacred; but rather a much simpler confrontation between the interests of the organised Churches and the freethinking approaches of non-credal traditions, the humanists and the liberal wings of all the major denominations?

My personal experience, confirmed by extensive study, indicates that there is no necessary contradiction between a rational approach to human problems and an honest, humble approach to the spiritual side of life. Difficulties arise only when some authority claims a monopoly on eternal truth – *eternal*, that is, until the next Vatican Council.

This is well illustrated by the notion of God (the Divine, the Godhead, the Absolute). Many modern writers have demonstrated how our ideas about the divine have evolved over the span of recorded history (and, presumably before that, but it is difficult to prove) in just the same way as have our ideas about the natural world, government, economics, justice and social organisation.

From animism through polytheism and monotheism we have arrived at the point where modern theologians define God in terms like *the ground of our being, ultimate reality,* or as a conceptual construct. From such positions it is the shortest of steps to the non-credal view that if there is an order of existence beyond the natural, then we cannot, by definition, know and say anything about it. That is not to say that there isn't an issue: people have been trying to get their brains around the notion of the ultimate nature of existence since we lived in caves, and they're not going to stop now. We have arrived at the point where *God* is not so much a definable entity as a convenient piece of shorthand to encompass that long-running debate.

A similar approach can be adopted to all the great religious and spiritual questions: ethics, forgiveness, sin, love/charity, prayer, death, afterlife and so on. Human beings have been wrestling with these ideas for as long as we have had language. We will most assuredly continue to do so, whatever the Churches and humanists may say. So why pretend that the debate ended two thousand years ago, or five hundred years ago, or that we are liable ever to arrive at final answers to such infinite questions?

While there will always be many opinions on these issues, is it beyond the capacity of modern, educated humans to be tolerant and respectful of the views of others so long as they don't try to impose them on their neighbours?

While the argument so far has been essentially intellectual, the implications are very practical. If the scriptural (or *revealed*) religions – for us, primarily, Christianity – could accept publicly what so many of their own theologians already accept privately (namely that their version of the truth is not the last word but, rather, just one more attempt by human beings in an agelong series of attempts to comprehend the place of human beings in the universal order of things), then we could move forward. We could arrive at a grown-up situation where all such attempts enjoy mutual respect and would be free to redefine themselves in the light of scientific and philosophical advances.

As things stand, Christianity and most of the other *revealed* faiths of the world are stuck in a particular period of cultural development, be it the early Chinese empire, the ancient civilisations of the Indus valley, the Golden Crescent of the pre-

Athenian Middle East, the Graeco-Roman era, the dramatic flowering of Arab culture in the sixth century, or the post-Renaissance of the sixteenth century.

As a result, their scriptures – and thus many of their beliefs – are couched in the language and metaphors of that period. In their different ways each tries to redefine their message to reflect the needs and intellectual perspectives of successive ages. However, in this they are severely handicapped by an insistence that the original scripture is an unchallengeable statement of the Divine. In an age of relativity, quantum theory and post-modernist thinking, such absolutist claims look increasingly improbable and unhelpful. All knowledge, all understanding, surely, is provisional and open to further refinement?

For their part, the secular humanists should acknowledge that there are, have always been, and very likely always will be, realms of human experience that go beyond rational analysis and prescription. *Religion*, in fact, has throughout history been an attempt by mankind to put all of their experience into some kind of explanatory framework. I see no good reason why humanism, rationalism, scepticism and free thought should not be seen as an integral part of that great human enterprise.

Just as religious traditions have had to take on board, however slowly and reluctantly, the thinking of ground-breaking scientists and philosophers – Indian, Greek, Arab and western European – so too today both Christians and humanists should accept the contemporary view of reality as an eclectic synthesis of science, philosophy and the subjective insights yielded by art, music, poetry, reflection and shared human experience.

This is in fact how most of us, including priests, ministers and rabbis, live in practice. So why not just admit it and discard the old absolutist pretensions? The great scriptures will always

have an honoured place as sources of great human wisdom and
of inspiration, but without any suggestion that any one of
them is the last word on the subject. This radical but simple
shift of perspective would allow the great religions, spiritual
and ethical traditions, to collaborate in many areas of modern
life. For those brought up in, and still comfortable with, the
Catholic tradition, all of the ancient liturgy and spiritual
practice could remain as a framework within which the human
business of living and coping goes on. For others, the Reformed
(Protestant) tradition is more meaningful and familiar. It too,
along with the Muslim, Hindu, Bahai'i, Buddhist and other
traditions, would offer alternative approaches to living in a
sane, fulfilling and satisfying way. And, of course, for the more
rational among us, the secular humanist tradition offers a less
subjective, less intuitive framework for living.

It is very probable in such a world that people would move,
as I have, from one spiritual tradition to another, as their
thinking, their values, and their spiritual insights develop.
Millions of others would die in the same tradition into which
they were born. More importantly, however, there would be
spiritual, emotional and philosophical support available to
everyone and all kinds of new, imaginative blends could
emerge. Personally, I would love to find and live within a
synthesis of oriental Tao and Buddhist thinking and Western
religious humanism.

Christianity in its early centuries represented one of
mankind's greatest spiritual advances. Its two thousand years of
history are studded with unparalleled achievements in the
realms of art, architecture, philosophy, music and social action,
as well as some very human lapses. If Christianity wants to
remain relevant to the needs of people in the twenty-first
century I am convinced it must take on board the
contemporary perspectives of humanism and transform itself

into a non-dogmatic, humane spiritual tradition firmly rooted
in the philosophical and religious history of Europe. This is
already happening among progressive, liberal Christians. But it
is without the blessing and acceptance of Church authorities.
Now, why might that be?

IN THE BEGINNING
WAS THE WORD

SEAN FREYNE

A CONFERENCE, held last year in the Chester Beatty Library, Dublin Castle, was intended to heighten awareness of one of the jewels in the crown of this remarkable collection of Oriental and Near Eastern art and artifacts. The Chester Beatty gospel papyri, or P45 to give them their official scholarly designation, form a substantial part of one of the earliest known codices of the four gospels, dating from the third century (c. AD 250). They are, therefore, a direct link with the Christian Church while it was still a persecuted sect within the Roman Empire. They put us in touch with the earliest period of a movement that was destined to shape so many facets of Western, and indeed global civilisation subsequently, though few could have anticipated this outcome at the time these documents were produced. The papyri are, then, cultural artifacts of the highest significance, of interest to the concerned secularist as well as objects worthy of respect for the committed Christian.

Like all artifacts from the past, the papyri too call for contextualisation within their own world if their significance for ours is to be properly assessed. As a Jewish reform movement, Jesus and the first Christians were heirs to the tradition of the Torah as a written collection of Israel's sacred writings. Yet, unlike some other Jewish movements of reform, such as the Essenes whose library is now known from the Dead Sea Scrolls, the early Christians were not primarily a scholastic community, at least originally.

The evangelist Luke presents Jesus reading from the scroll of the prophet Isaiah in the synagogue at Nazareth (Luke 4, 16-20), yet there is no evidence that he left any written records. Indeed his Pharisee opponents accused him of being 'unschooled' (John 7, 15). The earliest followers of Jesus are also described as being 'ignorant' and 'illiterate' (Acts of the Apostles 4,13). However, it is important to judge these statements as a later attempt at vilification by the small literate elite in Jerusalem, since a large part of ancient society belonged to an oral rather than a written culture, with no pejorative connotations. True, the apostle Paul used letter-writing as a way of communicating with the communities he had established in various cities, and a collection of his letters must have been made shortly after his death, an early version of which is also represented in the Chester Beatty collection (P46). The case of Paul indicates a shift in the social standing within an urban context of some at least of his new converts, as distinct from Jesus' own ministry, which was largely concentrated on the rural villagers of Galilee. Yet even Paul insists that his preference was for the spoken rather than the written word.

The impulse to produce a narrative account of Jesus' life and ministry was probably due to several factors – liturgical and catechetical needs; the death of the eye-witnesses to Jesus' life; and the shift from the Aramaic-speaking oral culture of Galilee, to the Greek speaking urban world of the Pauline mission. In this circle, history writing and biography were well-established literary genres, and thus it was necessary to produce 'an accurate account of all that has been accomplished among us, as these were handed on by those who from the beginning were eye-witnesses and ministers of the word' (Luke 1, 1-4). This statement echoes the literary practices of contemporary Graeco-Roman historians and no doubt helped to maintain the credibility of the movement among its pagan competitors. Unlike its Jewish precursors, however, the early Christians adopted the relatively novel form of the codex or book rather than the scroll, in publicising their message. This decision was for practical reasons such as convenience and portability for traveling missionaries, but it also helped to emphasise the movement's separate identity from the parent religion.

Modern scholarship has highlighted the fact that several different 'lives' of Jesus were produced with considerable variations even among the so-called synoptic gospels (i.e. Matthew, Mark and Luke), who shared a common pool of stories and sayings of Jesus that had circulated orally from the very beginning. John's gospel has always been recognised as being quite different in tone and emphasis, and others too were in circulation such as the gospels of Thomas, Peter and Mary, as well as gospels attributed to dissident groups such as the Ebionites and the Gnostics. The evidence points to the fact that the fourfold gospel, comprising our canonical ones, established itself relatively early as authoritative, probably because they were attributed to known disciples of Jesus (Matthew and John) or to those closely associated with that circle (Mark the interpreter of Peter and Luke the companion of Paul). It was this development that gave rise to the production of codices like the Chester Beatty one, containing the four gospels as well as Acts of the Apostles in the one book.

Despite some recent attempts to rehabilitate the other gospels as being early also, the likelihood is that they were derivative, and in several respects were regarded as not conforming to an emerging orthodoxy. Thus, towards the end of the second century, the gospel of Peter was in circulation in Antioch, and the local bishop, Serapion, allowed it for private reading but not for liturgical use in the Christian assembly.

The earliest commentators on this fourfold gospel, such as Justin Martyr (died *c.* AD 165) and Irenaeus of Lyon (died *c.* AD 200), were conscious of the differences between the individual accounts, possibly because pagan critics had sought to discredit them on the basis of these seeming discrepancies. Yet these first apologists stressed the deeper unity that existed between them, based on the one Spirit 'that bound them together.' Thus both writers prefer to speak of the Gospel rather than gospels (plural), and Irenaeus justifies the fourfold gospel by likening them to the four cardinal points of the compass, thereby implying the universality of the message they contained. This message was 'good news' about Jesus Christ as God's final word for the human family, a conviction that had driven the movement from its inception, as Paul had emphasised for his Galatian converts. There is only one gospel, he writes, and 'if I myself, or an angel from heaven were to preach another, we should be anathema' (Galatians 1, 8).

Others were less sure about the fourfold gospel and its unity as seen by Justin and Irenaeus. The Chester Beatty collection also contains another highly significant manuscript, the only extant version in the original Syriac of a commentary on a second century gospel harmony, the Diatessaron, which had been compiled by a Syrian monk, Tatian, about AD 175. He was apparently troubled by the discrepancies in the gospels, and sought to harmonise the four into one account (hence the Greek title of his work). His concerns were more historical than theological, probably because of his desire to present a single coherent account of the 'life' of Jesus to counteract the pagan despisers. This work was translated into various languages subsequently, but was particularly popular in Syria where it was replaced by the fourfold gospel only in the fifth century. Its importance lies in the fact that not all communities in the new movement, faced with the historical difficulties posed by the gospel differences, shared the theological conviction that lay behind the fourfold gospel. Tatian's concerns had to await the eighteenth-century Enlightenment's preoccupation with history before they would be addressed again, and indeed they are still very much at the centre of Gospel studies to this day.

There is, then, a seeming paradox at the heart of the early Christian self-understanding as this was expressed in the fourfold gospel. The good news is indeed one, yet its human expressions can be varied. The Word of God can never be exhausted or fully represented in the words of humans. It is for this reason that early Christian writers sought to compare the Scriptures with the Incarnation: one was the written Word of God, the other was the Word made flesh. Both modes, the written and the enfleshed, reveal and conceal the mystery of the divine love for the world. Human language, like human life, is always culturally and historically conditioned, partial and imperfect expressions of the deeper meaning of things. It calls for a special attuning of the ear to hear that deeper voice, the *lectio divina* of Christian worship and prayer.

The recognition of this surplus of meaning of the Christian story allowed Irenaeus and others after him to imagine the Christ in glory with four faces, each painted by a different evangelist. My own favourite expression of this profound idea is that of the thirteenth-century Window of the Evangelists at Chartres cathedral outside Paris. The central axis of the depiction consists of the virgin and child at the lower level (the Word made flesh), while the glorious risen Christ surrounded by the twelve apostles occupies the upper, rose section, directly above. On either side of the virgin and child are two panels, each containing a giant figure carrying a dwarf on his shoulders with an orientation towards the rose centre. What is utterly surprising about this portrayal is that the Evangelists are depicted as the dwarfs and the Old Testament prophets as the giants, inverting the usual Christian understanding of the New Testament being the fulfillment of the Old. The depiction gives expression to a famous medieval saying that 'we are like dwarfs on the shoulders of the giants of the past; we can see farther because we are raised higher.' In this particular application the pairing of evangelists and prophets allows each to see the Christ in a distinctive fashion. Despite the diversity of perspective that the different panels suggest, the whole window has a harmonious unity that encapsulates the one and fourfold gospel, and its indebtedness to its Israelite precursors.

In so far as we can ascertain, Christianity came to Ireland almost two centuries after the production, probably in Egypt, of the Beatty codex. By then the new movement had become the official religion of the empire, and the urgency was to spread the gospel to the very outer regions of the known world, even beyond the borders of the empire. In the library of Trinity College, at the other end of Dame Street from the Chester Beatty Library, the great uncial manuscript of the Book of Kells bears witness to this 'triumph' of Christianity with its elaborate illumination and highly decorative calligraphy. By contrast, the Beatty Codex was written in small script by a not very elegant hand and without any illumination. It is written on papyrus, not the more expensive vellum, and each sheet is folded in two to economise and fit the text of all four gospels into a single codex of manageable proportions. This contrast of style and execution between the two codices tells its own story of two very different moments of early Christian self-expression – the struggle for survival in a hostile environment and the high culture of triumphant Christendom.

At the beginning of the third millennium by Christian reckoning, Christendom, that is, the conjunction of Church and Empire in a single world, is now no longer a reality, even in Ireland, where, ironically, it survived longer than it did within its original boundaries in mainland Europe. As we search for ways of rescuing from the jaws of the Celtic Tiger some of the more important gospel values that shaped our culture, the moment from the past represented by the Beatty Codex has an important message. The pioneering spirit of those who produced this Christian codex and dared to live their lives by its challenging story could still serve us well today.

THE OLD ORDER CHANGETH

ANDREW GREELEY

LET US CONSIDER the condition of European religion at the end of the first millennium. The most likely scenarios for the future at that time would have been that Europe would become Muslim or Nordic or Slavic pagan. The Danes (Norse, Varangians, Vikings) were attacking Britain, Ireland, northern France, the Mediterranean countries, and what we now call the Ukraine. The Arabs had swept away the Christian countries of the Middle East and northern Africa and occupied most of Spain (where they had built a civilization unmatched anywhere in Western Europe).

The Saracens (as Christians called them) had occupied Sicily and periodically sacked Rome. The Papacy was dominated by the women of the Theophylact family and was in its worst condition ever. The 'Franks' had not been able to hold together the empire of Charlemagne and were having a difficult time imposing Catholicism on the Wends, the Lithuanians and the North Slavs. Byzantine Orthodoxy had enjoyed some progress among the South Slavs but had to contend with the pagan Bulgarians. No one would have bet on the survival of Christianity, save perhaps in far-off Ireland where the Danes were becoming Christian – and perhaps in scattered Irish monasteries on the continent. (Somehow they had managed to arrive in Moravia before Cyril and Methodius and in Kiev before Vladimir).

Thus the sociologist who dares to make projections about the Christian future in Europe treads cautiously. He would much rather project the present trends into the immediate future, save five or ten years. He garners a little more courage from the fact that the present trends seem rather firmly rooted in the past. Thus the end of organised religion, so cheerfully predicted by the wise men of the Enlightenment, seems so long overdue after a couple of centuries that there is no point in waiting for it.

In a recent study of twenty-three European nations conducted by the International Social Survey Programme, the majority of every nation except the Czech Republic and the former East Germany believed in God. In five of the countries – Cyprus, Ireland, Northern Ireland, Poland and Portugal – more than nine out of ten believe in God. In Italy, Spain, and Austria more than eight out of ten believe in God, and in Switzerland, Slovakia and Latvia seven out of ten are believers. (In Britain, the rate is 69 per cent). On the other hand, except in east Germany (51 per cent), atheists represent no more than a fifth of the population in any European nation. In twelve nations less than a tenth are atheists. In Russia, now in the midst of what may be the largest religious revival in human history, a third of the people say that once they didn't believe in God, but they now do.

In half of the nations the majority believes in religious miracles. Even in east Germany, where only 25 per cent believe in God, 39 per cent believe in religious miracles. If there is no God the question arises as to who works the religious miracles. Or perhaps the right question is, who is the God in whom the east Germans do not believe? (In Ireland 72 per cent believe in miracles, in Britain 42 per cent).

The picture that emerges out of these data is that God is alive and well in Europe, more alive in some countries than in others perhaps and the subject of serious devotion in only a few, but nonetheless still alive long after the Enlightenment is dead and buried – and cremated in the two Great Wars.

In seventeen of the countries, most people also believe in life after death. Moreover – and this is the most striking finding I will report in my book *Religion in Europe at the End of the Second Millennium* – in seventeen of the twenty-three countries the youngest birth cohorts (born since 1960) are more likely to believe in life after death than the earlier cohorts. In most cases a U-curve fits the data: the oldest and youngest cohorts are more likely to believe in life after death than the middle two cohorts. Grandparents and grandchildren are more likely to believe in human survival than parents. In six of the other countries (like Ireland, Poland and Cyprus) the level of belief is so high that there seems to be a ceiling on increase. Only in Britain is there a decrease in belief in life after death among the youngest cohort.

As I look at the U-curves I wonder if they do not reflect the impact of the Second World War – the lowest levels of hope in human survival are among the cohorts born during and immediately after the end of the war. More recently there is a return to what might be a relatively constant demand for hope, somewhere between 60 per cent and 70 per cent of the population anticipating human survival.

Magic survives in Europe too, save in those countries like Ireland and east Germany where there is relative certainty about the existence or the non-existence of God. In countries like the former West Germany, where there is relative uncertainty about God, there is a much higher rate of belief in good luck charms, faith healers, astrology, and fortune tellers. Moreover, in countries like the former West Germany, magic tends to blend with orthodox belief while in east Germany, and Ireland there is little such mixing. In none of the countries except east Germany do any less than a majority claim religious affiliation – though admittedly in some countries like Scandinavia this may be more of a civic than a religious affiliation. There are only four countries in which religious affiliation has significantly declined in the last decade, Ireland, England, Slovenia and Hungary (though only by four percentage points in Ireland).

In the three Catholic countries this decline can be accounted for by an increase during the decade of dissatisfaction with the behaviour of Church leadership. In England it may be that the appeal of Anglicanism is in a period of historic decline. The drop in confidence in Church leadership occurs in almost all of the nations studied, even in Russia where there has been a tremendous increase in Church affiliation. In virtually all the countries (including Poland, Italy, and Ireland) the traditional sexual and reproductive ethic is rejected by substantial to overwhelming majorities.

Thus in Europe at the end of the second millennium and the beginning of the third (January 1, 2001), belief in God is stable, belief in life after death is increasing among the young, magic persists as does Church affiliation, confidence in Church leaders declines and the traditional sexual teaching can no longer be enforced. The continent is by no means devout (if it ever were, which seems unlikely) but religion survives.

When I tell people that I'm working on a book about religion in Europe at the end of the millennium, many of my colleagues are surprised. Isn't religion completely dead in Europe? It is fair to say, I think, that this is an assumption, almost a dogma in the universities of Europe and America (though there is surprisingly little correlation between university attendance and religious decline). I cite the Russian religious revival and say that God is alive and well and has been hiding in the Moscow Metro. However, the lesser religious revivals in the other former socialist countries (including an increase in belief in life after death even among the young in east Germany) and the persistence of religion in other countries, especially the Catholic countries, also call into question the dogma of the death of religion.

It will come eventually, say the surviving believers in the doctrines of the Enlightenment from Voltaire to Durkheim. When, I ask. In face of the data they rarely are willing to guess. Voltaire, I observe, died a quarter of a millennium ago and religion still slogs along, however imperfectly and however much below its own ideals. Why? The reason I think is that humans (maybe two thirds of them) tend to need something to believe in and something to belong to, some kind of meaning and some sort of belonging, something to explain both life and death and a heritage to pass on to their children. Hence my very cautious projections for the third millennium in Europe:

1) Religion will survive. Human kind will continue to believe, perhaps hesitantly and not without doubt, in God.

2) Belief in life after death will survive. Faced with an alternative between Macbeth's 'tale told by an idiot' and Teilhard de Chardin's 'something is afoot in the universe, something that looks like gestation and birth', humankind will continue to tilt, however uncertainly, towards the latter option.

3) Magic will also survive, because humans want certainty, which is more than just hope.

4) The main religious heritages – Catholic, Protestant, Orthodox, Islamic – will also survive and perhaps, only perhaps, come closer together. Catholicism may have the greatest resources of imagination and story, but there is no reason at present to believe that those resources mean much to the clergy and the hierarchy, not as much as the power they do not want to give up.

5) The Churches will no longer be able to control the private behaviour of their members. People will decide their own terms for affiliation.

6) Eventually – heaven knows when – religious leaders will learn that it is no longer enough to give orders. They must also learn to listen.

7) There will also be – again no predictions – a turn away from the authoritarian centralism in Church governance in the past centuries and a return to the more democratic and pluralistic styles of governance of the first millennium.

8) Theologians and Church leaders, and especially theologians who are Church leaders, may learn that it is not enough to describe a problem theologically to solve it, but don't bet too much on that.

These are very modest projections based either on the data or on the obvious implications of the data. They suggest that the present situation, in which people cling to faith by their finger tips with little help from clergy or theologians, however unstable it might be, could also constitute the 'normal' condition for religion in our era and the eras immediately to come.

After that, I leave predictions to the visionaries, to the seers and to those who hear whispers in the night. I have said nothing about the social and environmental and global issues with which many of the religious elite are concerned. I have simply no data to estimate the extent to which these concerns are likely to permeate the religious population in the years ahead. None of the four religions of the book have figured out yet what will replace the missionary impulse of the last several centuries or even if it should be replaced.

There is, I realised, something depressingly dull and unexciting about my projections. They are gray, problematic, and sound like too much of more of the same thing. Such, I submit, is the nature of reality, especially the short-run reality with which we sociologists must deal. Yet there will also surely appear in the third millennium marvels that no one anticipates as well as tragedies that no one fears. God keeps his surprises to Himself.

PART TWO

A BRIEF HISTORY OF CHRISTIANITY

Patrick Comerford

TIME AND ETERNITY

Over the past two thousand years, Christianity has played a vital role in Western culture. Art, science, music, architecture and literature have drawn on religion to such an extent that Christianity has formed many of our cultural ideas, symbols, rituals and political ideals. The Irish theologian, Professor Richard Hanson, has pointed out: 'As a religion, Christianity has both formed history and has been formed by history.' Christianity has always had good reason to emphasise the study of its own history. 'The Christian religion, above all others, is concerned with the relationship of time and eternity,' Sir Steven Runciman of Cambridge has written. 'Its central doctrine, the Incarnation, is not only an eternal truth but an event in history; it is a bridge between the temporal and the eternal.'

Christianity claims to have originated in a series of historical events, which, to varying degrees, are normative for its message and its significance. The study of Christianity could never be limited to the study of the Bible and the life of Christ alone. The Church decided which books were canonical – or part of the Bible – and which books to exclude from the tradition. As the Church of Ireland Bishop of Meath and Kildare, Most Rev. Richard Clarke, has pointed out, 'there is a very important sense in which [Christ] did not found the Church'. Jesus preached the Kingdom of God, and the Church was founded on His teachings.

The Bible and tradition run parallel with the story of the Church in shaping Christian experience. And so, the story of Christianity over the past two thousand years is not only another branch of history, but an important component in theology. According to Professor Runciman, Church history needs objective study, intuitive sympathy, imaginative perception, and a comprehension of 'the fears and aspirations and convictions that have moved past generations.'

Traditionally, the history of Christianity has focused on saints and missionaries, rather than providing an independent interpretation of religious behaviour. This apologetic tendency was strengthened in the middle of the twentieth century by theologians who wrote as though human history had no meaning at all after the death and Resurrection of Jesus Christ. Today, no Church historian would seek to justify many of the experiences of past generations in the Church. Who would seek to defend the Crusades, the Inquisition or those Christians whose anti-Semitism was a constituent part of the political culture and climate leading to the Holocaust? Church history seeks to place these events in their context and to understand the contribution of other forces and the social, political, economic and cultural circumstances of the times.

It becomes more difficult to appreciate the contexts of events closer to our own lives. Will future generations see the missionaries of the last century as enlightened advocates of the social gospel, seeking to combat the worst extremes of imperial exploitation and indigenous superstition, or as agents of colonialism? Will future generations looking at twentieth-century South Africa judge the Churches for their resistance to apartheid, or the contribution of the Dutch Reformed Churches to formulating apartheid? Will future historians looking at the Irish Church of today emphasise the growth of the ecumenical movement, or sectarian bigotry?

Taking stock of two thousand years of Christianity takes us through the conversion of the Roman empire and the formulation of Christian doctrine; the expansion of Christianity – often thanks to the journeys of Irish missionaries; the great schism that divided Christendom, East and West; the rise of Islam, the Crusades, and the collapse of the Byzantine Empire; the invention of movable type and the translation of the Bible; Luther, Calvin, the Reformation, the Counter Reformation and the Renaissance; the Pilgrim Fathers and the move to guarantee religious freedom and the separation of Church and State; the growth of the modern missionary movement and the abolition of slavery through the energy of evangelicals; the challenge to faith posed by Darwin, Marx, Nietzsche and Freud; the murder of six million Jews in the Holocaust; and the 1960s, when Pope John XXIII convened Vatican II and Martin Luther King led the Civil Rights Movement.

The 1960s also saw the Church and theology challenged by the concepts of the 'Death of God' and 'post-Christianity'. By the end of the twentieth century, we reach a Church that continues to grow phenomenally in the 'Two-Thirds' world, reinvigorated in part by liberation theologies, but challenged by a resurgent Islam. But in the older Christian heartlands, were liturgical reform and debates about ethics, sexual morality and the ordination of women signs of a Church that was finding new life and renewing itself, and was the Church capable of confronting decline and secularism?

MANY DIVERSIONS ALONG 'THE WAY'

The early history of the Church is still part of the New Testament story, and the canon of the New Testament and Church doctrines did not take their present form until long after the Apostolic Church. Traditionally, Pentecost is seen as the birth of the Church, but despite the reports in the Acts of the Apostles of early mass conversions after Pentecost, the followers of Jesus Christ remained a small group or sect within Judaism, alongside the Pharisees, Sadducees and Essenes, until two decisive events turned their faith into a mass movement: the conversion of Paul, and the destruction of Jerusalem.

Paul's conversion on the road to Damascus is such a decisive event that in a real sense he might be said to be the founder of the Church. The name Christian was first applied to a group of believers in Antioch, and Christianity quickly spread through Damascus and Antioch, the capital of Syria and third city of the Empire, and on through Syria, Cilicia and Asia Minor.

Later tradition would associate many Churches with the early Apostles: Alexandria with Mark, both Antioch and Rome with Peter, Byzantium and the Scythians with Andrew, and Phrygia in Asia Minor with Philip – even the Church in Persia and on the Malabar coast of India would claim it was founded by the Apostle Thomas.

The spread of early Christianity was due in part to the exodus of Jewish Christians to Asia Minor during the Jewish War in the years AD 66 to 70. But the first real missionary endeavours of the new movement were launched by Paul, whose journeys saw the Church expand throughout the Eastern Mediterranean in what we know today as Cyprus, Turkey, Greece, into Malta, present-day Italy, and (perhaps) as far west as Spain.

The earliest followers of 'The Way' were recruited in the synagogues, among the Jews of the Diaspora, and among ethical, monotheistic Gentiles who worshipped with Jews. For both groups, koine Greek was the common language, and their thoughts were shaped by the thinking of Plato and Aristotle. The sack of Jerusalem in the year 70 marked the end of the dominance of Jewish Christians in the Church. Gentiles, who had achieved equality in the Church through Paul's endeavours, now became the dominant Christians, and the focus switched from Jerusalem to the capital of the Gentile world, Rome.

The bridge between the New Testament story and Church history is provided by the writers known collectively as the Apostolic Fathers, including Justin Martyr and the author of *Clement* at the end of the first century, and Polycarp of Smyrna and the authors of the *Didache*, at the beginning of the second century.

Justin Martyr, who was born of Greek parents in Palestine, saw a continuity between his Christian faith and his Greek philosophical past, and anchored his Christian faith in his Greek heritage. Polycarp, who is said to have known John the Divine, the author of the Book of Revelations, was the last living link between the Apostolic Church of the New Testament and the historic church of the Apostolic Fathers.

With the letter known as 'I Clement', written from Rome to Corinth around the year AD 96, we begin to glimpse common patterns emerging in the liturgy, life and ministry of the Church at the end of the first century. A clearer pattern of Church order and ministry is defined in the early second century by Ignatius of Antioch in his writings. As he was being taken to Rome to be martyred, he wrote seven letters setting out the threefold pattern of bishop, priest and deacon, with the local bishop as the focus of unity in the face of schism and heresy.

By the beginning of its second century, Christianity was under attack, internally and externally, from a number of diverse, competing sects known collectively as Gnostics, who claimed access to secret knowledge (*gnosis*). For Gnostics, the spirit was good and the flesh was evil, and they believed in a remote supreme god, sometimes identified with the God of the Old Testament but who was disengaged from the world.

The first firm challenge to heresy within the early Church came from Irenaeus, the author of *Against Heresies*. A Greek who had learned at the feet of Polycarp before moving to Lyons, he became the first bishop in Gaul (France).

The challenge from Gnosticism and other heresies also led to the Church agreeing on the canon of Scripture, deciding which books were to be included and which excluded from an accepted Bible. Irenaeus was among the first to talk about a New Testament scripture alongside the Old Testament. Apostolic teaching, handed down through successive generations, and apostolic scripture, in the agreed books, amounted to the common apostolic tradition shared by an increasingly diffuse and diverse Church, now scattered throughout the empire and beyond.

The challenge of heresy and schism also marks the beginning of theology, and Tertullian, the North African who died in AD 220, is regarded as the father of Latin, western theology, although he later became disillusioned with the mainstream Church. North Africa produced other great theologians at the turn of the second and third century, including Clement of Alexandria, Origen (also born in Alexandria), and Cyprian, the martyr bishop of Carthage.

Apart from heresy and schism, the Church also faced regular persecution, often for the refusal of Christians to take part in the emperor cult, to swear oaths or serve in the imperial army, but also because of widespread vulgar charges, originating in eucharistic practice and the teaching of Christian love, that Christians indulged in cannibalism and incest. During the severe persecution under Marcus Aurelius in AD 177, Tertullian could comment with sarcasm: 'If the Tiber rises too high or the Nile too low, the cry is "The Christians to the lion". All of them, to a single lion?' Despite persecution and martyrdom, Tertullian observed, 'the blood of the martyrs is the seed of the Church.'

The Church was thriving, and missionary, social and intellectual advances were preparing the way that would lead to the conversion of the Emperor Constantine at the beginning of the fourth century, the accommodation of the Church with temporal power, and the consolidation of Church teachings at the great ecumenical councils in the decades that followed.

But the old heresies, schisms and battles would not go away. The theories and beliefs of Gnostics and Arians would continue to resurface in the Church in successive generations, and they continue to appear today. The rift between the Greek East and Latin West would widen throughout the remaining centuries of the first millennium, so that the Church, despite winning the internal battle for orthodoxy, could never succeed in maintaining its unity or a common Church order. The divisions of the twenty-first century can be traced back to the seeds sown in the first, second and third centuries of Church history.

A RIFT BETWEEN EAST AND WEST

With the conversion of Constantine in AD 312, and his subsequent victory at the Battle of the Milvian Bridge near Rome, the imperial persecution of Christians came to an end. Christians were guaranteed freedom of religion, Church goods and property were restored, Sunday became a special day, the Church was free to expand its mission work, and there was a rapid growth in Church membership. But the new freedoms also allowed the growth of internal dissension and heresies, more complex Church structures were demanded to cope with both expansion and dissent, and the new footing for Church-State relations also gave the State more say in Church affairs.

The first major doctrinal controversy arose in the debate over the Trinity and the teachings of a Libyan theologian, Arius, who taught that the Son was not co-equal and co-essential with the Father, but merely the chief of his creations, that the two persons were substantially similar rather than of the same substance. In an attempt to settle the dispute, Constantine used his powers as emperor to call and preside over the first of the great Councils of the Church. The Council of Nicaea, attended by three hundred or so bishops, agreed on formulas that later gave us the Nicene Creed.

Meanwhile, as the Church was reaching a new understanding with the state and the world, Anthony of Egypt and other leading Christian intellectuals and writers were leaving the cities and towns to live on their own in the desert. The Greek word *monos* (alone) gave us the words monk and monastery to describe how these hermits lived, and the monastic tradition would become a mainstay of Church life and mission for centuries to come.

In the Eastern Empire, Athanasius, John Chrysostom, Basil, and Gregory Nazianzus came to be counted as the four Doctors of the Eastern Church or great founding theologians. Athanasius was Bishop of Alexandria, but was forced into exile on a number of occasions by the Arians. Unbowed, he was the biographer of Anthony of Egypt, and so introduced monasticism to the West at a time when the rift between East and West was increasing. For the first time, he listed the contents or canon of the New Testament as we now know it. Two years after his death, his supporters and the Cappadocian Fathers, including Basil and Gregory, eventually triumphed in 381 in the doctrinal debate at the Council of Constantinople. The creed agreed at

Constantinople, now known as the Nicene Creed, remains the standard test of orthodox teaching and doctrine.

The first breach between Rome and the four other patriarchal sees in the East came when John Chrysostom (347–407) was deposed as Patriarch of Constantinople in 403. For eleven years, between 404 and 415, there was no communion between Rome and Constantinople – a foretaste of future, deeper divisions in later centuries.

During that time, the Goths sacked Rome in AD 410. With the collapse of the Roman Empire at the start of the fifth century, new foundations were needed if Christianity were to be a world force. Jerome (342–420), who moved to Bethlehem, produced a readable Bible translated into the common language, Latin (hence the Vulgate). In North Africa, Augustine (354–430), Bishop of Hippo, addressed the doubts of a shaken Church with his *Confessions* and *The City of God*, and provided the West with a theology that could survive the centuries. Jerome and Augustine, along with Ambrose and Gregory, would be counted among the four Latin Doctors of the Church. Later, a rediscovery of Augustine would inspire both the Reformers and the Catholic Counter-Reformation.

Having dealt with Arianism at Nicaea and Constantinople, the Church called another great council at Ephesus in 431 to deal with arguments about the Virgin Mary and her role as *Theotokos* or 'Bearer of God'. The deposed Patriarch of Constantinople, Nestorius, was condemned as a heretic. In the face of efforts by the Emperor Theodosius to reverse the decisions, the monks of Constantinople marched through the streets to support the bishops of the council, and the decision was endorsed in Rome by the Pope.

Today, the arguments of the four great councils may appear to be obscure philosophy, but they identified the fundamental issues central to the Christian faith: Jesus Christ is not merely a super creature or the last great prophet sent by God, but in his deity is the foundation of all true Christian faith and he is the one, unique revelation of God.

Amid the gloom prevailing in the middle of the fifth century, Pope Leo the Great (440–461) assumed the imperial title of Pontifex Maximus (Supreme Priest), declared his words to be the word of Peter, influenced the decisions of the Council of Chalcedon in 451, and set to putting the Church of Rome on a new footing.

Leo the Great was a contemporary of Patrick, who is said to have arrived in Ireland as a missionary bishop in AD 431 and continued his missionary work until his death (c. 460). Patrick and the early Celtic Church built on the pre-Patrician Church in Ireland, and then, beginning with the foundation of a monastery by Columcille (Columba) in Iona in 563, the first Celtic missionaries brought new life first to Scotland and a dwindling Church left behind in Britain after the collapse of the Western Roman Empire, and then into northern Europe. The Celtic monks were breathing new life into the Church in northern Europe, while in southern Europe Benedict was drawing up a Rule that would reform monastic rule throughout the West.

In the East, the Emperor Justinian (527–565) had re-established Byzantium's territorial control, combated a resurgent Arianism followed by the barbarian kings, and in the space of six years built the great church of Haghia Sophia, the supreme expression of the Byzantine genius. In the West, a recovering papacy under Gregory the Great sent Augustine as first Archbishop of Canterbury in 597. But Christianity in the East and West was ill-prepared for the newest challenge about to face it: the rise of Islam. Muhammad, who was born in 570, established his new system in Mecca in 622. The new religion would reflect many of the conflicts Christianity had tried to suppress, including Arianism and the arguments over images and icons.

CHRISTENDOM COMES UNDER ATTACK

The four great ecumenical councils of the Church defined orthodox Christian doctrine for succeeding generations, but they failed to bring peace to the empire, to end dissension, or to keep external threats at bay. The main heresies dealt with at the councils were those of the Arians and the Monophysites. Until Egypt and Syria fell to the Muslims, the Monophysites provided a rallying point for anti-imperial forces in the non-Hellenistic (Greek) populations, while in the west, contrary to later misconceptions, the Barbarians waiting at the gates were not pagans, but followers of the Arian heresy.

In AD 410, when the Goths sacked Rome, comparisons were drawn with the Horsemen of the Apocalypse. Pope Leo I succeeded in persuading Attila the Hun to turn back from Rome, but Genseric the Vandal could only be persuaded to refrain from setting fire to the city as the Vandals spent a fortnight looting its riches. The last Roman Emperor of the West, Romulus Augustulus, was deposed by Odoacer, the Germanic warrior, who in 476 became the first Barbarian king of Rome.

The new Rome no longer held any political claims over the old Rome, and was finding it difficult to maintain any religious claims over it too. East and West were increasingly divided, and the new *filioque* clause – defining the Holy Spirit as proceeding from both the Father and the Son – was soon introduced into the Nicene Creed in the West, an innovation that would prove a major stumbling block in East/West dialogue for centuries to follow. Theoretically, Theodoric, the Ostrogoth king of Rome, was subject to the Emperor, but he suspected the philosopher Boethius of dealing with the king's enemies in Constantinople and had him arrested, tortured, and executed in Pavia in 524. Boethius has been described as the last Roman and the first scholastic.

Although death destroyed his plans to translate Plato and Aristotle into Latin and deprived the West of the wisdom of Greek philosophy for generations, he provided the materials for early scholastic theology and even anticipated some of its methods. In *The Consolation of Philosophy* Boethius asked questions that still remain relevant in theology today: how can evil exist in the world if God is really good? How can we reconcile God's foreknowledge with human freewill?

The death of Boethius and the loss of classical philosophy would mean that, for Western Europe, the first part of the Middle Ages was truly the Dark Ages. Western Europe would soon come under attack in the west and south from Islam through Spain, and in the north from the Vikings of Scandinavia. But all was not as dark as it seemed: Christianity was flourishing and prospering in Ireland in the far west, and in Byzantium in the east, and from those centres would come lights to lighten the Dark Ages.

In 563, Colmcille or Columba founded his monastery in Iona, and from there Christianity spread throughout Scotland and northern England. In 585, Columbanus travelled from Bangor to found monasteries at Annegray and Luxeuil in France, at Saint Gall in Switzerland, and as far south as Bobbio in Italy. In 635, Aidan established Lindisfarne, and Aidan's pupil, Hilda, later established her foundation at Whitby.

In the East, an anonymous Syrian monk was producing works that would be later ascribed to Dionysius the Areopagite. His emphasis on God's utter transcendence would permeate Eastern Orthodox theology with its 'via negativa' or 'apophatic' approach, in which God is talked about not by saying what he is, but by saying what he is not.

While Christianity flourished in the East, however, Christendom was under attack on many fronts: the Persians were harrying the Empire, and the Vandal Arians were sweeping across North Africa, threatening both the religious and political order. The Emperor Justinian tried to reconquer and rebuild his Empire, symbolised physically in the year 532 with the triumphant rebuilding of Aghia Sophia, the great church of Constantinople.

A century later, in 632, Muhammad died, and soon the Muslims had captured Syria and Jerusalem (638), Egypt (639–642), and much of North Africa (643). As Islam was on the march, the Eastern Church survived the 'robber councils' and the stormy debates that sought compromise with the Monophysites. Although Maximus the Confessor (580–662) was tortured and exiled for his beliefs, he became the most significant theologian of the seventh century and was later hailed as 'the real father of Byzantine theology'.

The persuasive strength of Eastern Orthodox theology triumphed at the sixth ecumenical council of the church, the third Council of Constantinople (680–681). The council marked the last attempt to compromise with the Monophysites; the heresy of monotheletism was condemned and Pope Agatho accepted the condemnation of an earlier predecessor as a heretic in the terms: 'We define that there shall be expelled from the holy church of God and anathematised Honorius, who was once pope of Old Rome.'

The ruling was accepted, but the divisions deepened. Eventually, Pope Leo III would distance himself completely from the Emperor in the East, encouraging rebellion among the monks of Constantinople and crowning Charlemagne as Holy Roman Emperor in Rome on Christmas Day. Nevertheless, the theologians of the East would continue to influence and teach their counterparts in the West.

The 'last of the Greek Fathers' was John of Damasacus (c. 675–c. 749), the son of a senior official in the court of the caliph. A strong defender of icons during the iconoclastic controversy, he gathered together the earlier teachings of the fathers into a systematic manual and continues to influence and often shape thinking in all sections of the Church.

In the West, the Greek Fathers also influenced theology during the Carolingian renaissance through the one truly original thinker of the Dark Ages, the Irish monk, John Scotus Erigena (c. 810–c. 877). Scotus was, perhaps, the greatest intellectual of his day, and one of the few people in the West at the time to know Greek.

Through his translation of *Dionysius the Areopagite* and his commentary on Maximus the Confessor, Scotus influenced much medieval mysticism, and shaped later medieval theology, including the work of Thomas Aquinas. It could be said Irish monks had brought Christianity to northern Europe in the sixth and seventh century, and through Scotus they shaped Western intellectual life for the centuries that followed.

THE CRUEL FIGHT FOR THE HOLY LAND

When Islam was dislodged from France and receded into Spain, Western Christendom began to think about lost lands at the other end of the Mediterranean. The subsequent Crusades, however, left a bitter legacy both in relations between the Churches of the East and the West and between Islam and Christianity.

As Europe and the Church emerged from the Dark Ages at the close of the first millennium, the arguments and divisions of earlier centuries had taken hold, and Christianity was no longer united. Dissenters, including the Monophysites and Nestorians, had been condemned at earlier councils, and had been marginalised by the Church. In the face of the onward march of Islam, Christianity was further divided and weakened by the Great Schism of 1054, brought about by the West's introduction of the *filioque* to the Nicene Creed, and Eastern resistance to the intractable claims of Papal supremacy.

The relationship between Christianity and Islam since the Middle Ages is often seen in the West in terms of military conflict, particularly the Arab conquest of the Holy Land rather than the Crusades, and in the East in terms of the Arab contribution to Western culture, including architecture, mathematics and the preservation of Greek philosophy and medicine. But from a Western perspective, it is often forgotten that Islam managed initially to incorporate Christian communities successfully into Muslim society, while Christian Europe continues to fail in its attempts to accommodate Muslims within Christendom. However, today's antagonism does not reflect earlier relations between Christians and the Arabic-speaking world.

Prior to the rise of Islam, the settled Arabs of the Roman East were rapidly assimilated into the empire. By the third to fifth centuries, Christianity had become widely accepted among Arabs. Under the tutelage of the Arab client kings of Byzantium and imperial administrators, Arabic was elevated from a spoken language to a literary language, and a distinctly Arab Christian culture developed in the fifth and sixth centuries, with Arab bishops, Arab saints, and, perhaps, Arabic liturgy and religious poetry.

In 637, however, five years after the death of Muhammad, the Patriarch Sophronius surrendered Jerusalem to Caliph Umar, and less than two years later died of a broken heart. In the city that was once the very heart of Christianity, the Dome of the Rock was built with the skills and crafts of Christian artisans, some from as far afield as Constantinople. Christians in the East soon learned, at a cost, how to live with their Muslim conquerors.

The early Christians considered Islam a Christian heresy, while Muslims saw Christianity as an heretical distortion corrected by Islam. The great theologian John of Damascus (c. 660–749), had been a childhood friend of the future Umayyad caliph, al-Yazid. He had a discerning knowledge of the Qu'ran, and argued that Islam was a heresy formed through Muhammad's ill-assorted contact with Christians and Arians. Indeed, Islam addresses a number of debates current in Christianity at the time, including the unity of God, the nature of Jesus, the controversy over images and icons in worship, and the place and role of priesthood.

In the century coinciding with the Umayyad rule, no fewer than five Syrians and three Greeks – refugees fleeing from Islam – became Popes in Rome, but Islamic rule in the lands at the heart of the Bible story caused no fear in Western Christendom while those rulers were Arabs. The West was stunned by the ravages in Jerusalem by the Caliph al-Hakim in 1010, but the military response to the Islamic presence in the Holy Land came only after the Great Schism in 1054 and following the capture of Jerusalem by the Seljuk Turks in 1076.

The first Crusade was proclaimed by Pope Urban II at the Council of Clermont in 1095 with the object of securing the safety of pilgrims travelling to Jerusalem. Antioch was captured in 1098, Jerusalem was taken in 1099 and Godfrey was crowned King of Jerusalem in 1100. During the next twenty years, scores of Latin states were established in Syria and Palestine, and the Crusaders' Latin Kingdom lasted until 1187.

The Second Crusade, provoked by the fall of Edessa in 1144 and proclaimed by Bernard of Clairvaux in 1147, ended in failure in 1187 with the capture of Jerusalem by Saladin, who was neither an Arab nor a Turk but a Kurdish chieftain. The Third Crusade (1189–1192) failed to recapture Jerusalem, while the Fourth Crusade (1202–1204) was diverted to Constantinople with the approval of Pope Innocent in an effort to assert papal claims to universal primacy. Christians rather than Muslims had become the enemies of the Crusades, the new Rome was sacked and the Emperor and the Patriarch fled. The Latin Empire, however, eventually collapsed in 1261 after the French, Flemish, German, Venetian and Genoese Crusaders and conquerors fought each other.

During the fifth Crusade, Francis of Assisi had a famous encounter with Saladin's nephew at Damiettea, when he prayed for the Sultan and disavowed the sword. The Crusades remained a Papal obsession, however, and Crusaders were granted indulgences and given the status of martyrs in the event of death in battle, penances at home were lifted, debts remitted and pardons pledged.

As the Crusades petered out and the papacy came to accept that the Holy Land was to remain in Muslim hands, canon lawyers for the first time began to discuss human rights and the protection of minorities. Nevertheless, the Crusades left a bitter and lasting legacy. There was the obscenity of the Children's Crusade in 1212, and the cruelty of the crusades against heretics, especially the Albigenses in southern France. In the east, the Crusades left a permanent trauma in the psyche of Arab Christians, who were treated better under the rule of Muslim Arabs and Turks than they were by Latin Crusaders, and who continue to suffer from the Western equation of Arab with Muslim.

When the Turks under Sultan Muhammad II captured Constantinople in 1453, almost four centuries after the Great Schism had divided the Orthodox East and the Latin West, the divisions among Christians appeared to have been sealed. Pius II died in 1464, having failed to organise a further Crusade. Western Christianity, having long abandoned early Christian pacifism, would take a long time to recover from the bloodshed it had inflicted and to develop theories of the just war and

human rights. Bishop Kenneth Cragg says that Western
Christianity, 'in cherishing the sacrament of places . . . cruelly
betrayed the sacrament of communities.'

Today's most bitter legacy of the Crusades is that Christians
and Muslims, who tried to understand each other with
intellectual honesty at the time of John of Damascus, often
remain enemies in many parts of the world, from the
Philippines to Lebanon and Sudan.

THE CRUSADING THEOLOGY OF PHILOSOPHY

The Crusades, which marked a dark period in the history of
Christianity, dominated the Church's external relations from
the end of the eleventh century until the middle of the fifteenth
century. With their brutality, misdirection and violent
conquests, and the lust for power and expansion that they
engendered, the Crusades damaged the Church's relations with
the Jewish and Muslim worlds, if not irreparably then at least
until the late twentieth century. Their legacy also served to seal
the rift between the Orthodox Church of the East and the Latin
Church of the West.

Yet, despite this stain on the heritage of Christianity,
internally the Latin Church of the West was lifting itself out of
the Dark Ages. Once again, the joys of philosophy were being
rediscovered, and expressed in the writings of great Christian
thinkers such as Anselm, Bernard, Peter of Lombard, and,
uniquely, Thomas Aquinas. At the same time, the monastic
orders were being challenged by the reforming zeal of the
Cistercians, while new orders such as the Franciscans and
Dominicans were challenging many of the weaknesses
corrupting the Church. And fresh stirrings and new ideas from
Peter Abelard, the Waldensians and John Wycliffe were a hint
at, or foretastes of, the great movement that would soon
challenge the institutionalised Church through the
Reformation.

At the time the first Crusade was being proclaimed, the Archbishop of Canterbury was the former Benedictine Abbot of Bec, Anselm (c. 1033–1109), who spent most of his reign in exile on the Continent. Anselm was the first truly great theologian of the mediaeval West, and is sometimes described as the founder of scholasticism. He followed Augustine's method of 'faith seeking understanding' and allowed philosophy to play a significant, if limited, role in theology.

In his *Proslogion* Anselm presented his famous 'ontological argument' for the existence of God. Today, it would be easy to accuse him of attempting to define God into existence, but despite their weaknesses Anselm's arguments are impressive for their day. He sought to show how reasonable faith is, rather than to offer a strict proof of it and he succeeded in bringing theology back to the level of debate it had lost since the days of Gregory the Great five hundred years earlier.

Bernard of Clairvaux (1090–1153), who preached around Europe raising support for the second Crusade, had first entered the new Cistercian monastery of Clairvaux to flee the world, but became one of the most widely travelled and active leaders of the Western Church in the twelfth century. The last great representative of the early medieval tradition of monastic theology, Bernard has been called 'the Last of the Fathers'. He was a strong opponent of Peter Abelard and the Waldensians, and with equal vigour defended the claims of the Papacy. He also warned against the dangers of papal tyranny however. 'It seems to me you have been entrusted with stewardship over the world, not given possession of it,' he told Pope Eugenius III. 'There is no poison more dangerous for you, no sword more deadly than the passion to rule.'

Bernard's contemporary, Peter Lombard (c. 1100–1160), who died as Bishop of Paris, was the author of the *Sentences*, which became the standard textbook of theology. Writing a commentary on his *Sentences* became a regular part of the preparation for a doctorate in theology, and it was generations before his work was superseded by the *Summa Theologica* of Thomas Aquinas.

Thomas Aquinas (1225–1274) spent most of his life teaching at Paris, where the burning issue was how theology should respond to the rediscovery of Aristotle. His contemporary, Bonaventure (1221–1274), kept to the traditional Platonist worldview, while Thomas tried to conduct a synthesis between reason and faith, philosophy and theology, Aristotle and Christianity. His *Summa Theologica* was written in the last ten years of his life, and it took some centuries for it to replace Peter Lombard's *Sentences* as the standard textbook for Western theology. Despite a decline in Thomas' influence in recent decades, his work remains the greatest achievement of scholastic theology, and his method of reasoning and approach to philosophy has influenced subsequent generations of philosophers, including Marx.

His spiritual greatness should not be forgotten either however: near the end of his life, he had a vision while saying Mass that caused him to stop writing; he stated that compared with what had then been revealed to him, all that he had written seemed like straw.

Many of his contemporaries were equally humble, and denied they had contributed any original thoughts to the fields of theology or philosophy. These great men, in their humility, believed they were simply building on the works and writings of their predecessors, or, in the words of Bernard of Chartres: 'We are like dwarves sitting on the shoulders of giants.'

Apart from their writings, however, which influenced theology and philosophy for centuries after, Bonaventure, Thomas and Bernard also represented three new forms of monastic life that continue to shape the spirituality of the church: Bernard was instrumental in the spread of the Cistercians, who sought to reform the Benedictine tradition; Thomas was a member of the Order of Preachers, the Dominicans founded in 1216 by Dominic (1170–1221); while Bonaventure was Minister General of the Franciscans, founded by Francis of Assisi (1181–1266). However, not all the great spiritual writers of the day were men. In recent years there has been a renewed interest in the writings of the English mystic and anchoress, Julian of Norwich (c. 1342– after 1413).

Despite the cruelty of the Crusades, and the relentless pursuit of dissent in the shape of the Albigensians and the Waldensians, the spirituality of Julian and of Thomas à Kempis, the theology of Aquinas and the poverty of Dominic and Francis point to a Christianity that continued to develop new riches and thinking.

Although the integrity of the Western Church was weakened by the Crusades and its claims further weakened by the Avignon captivity of the Papacy (1309–1377), Western Christianity was alive intellectually and spiritually.

The questioning faith of Peter Abelard in France in the twelfth century, the Waldensians in Italy and further afield in the thirteenth century, and of John Wycliffe and the Lollards in England in the fourteeth century were nurtured in a Church that would soon find itself ripe for the challenges posed by both the Reformation and the Counter-Reformation.

DECAY PAVES THE WAY FOR THE REFORMATION

Despite the efforts of Francis of Assisi and others to call the Church to reform, by the fifteenth century the Church had become totally identified with the interests of the State and power, and the very notion of Christendom made the powers of Church and State inseparable.

Those who challenged the status quo faced being marginalised or condemned as heretics. The fifteenth-century

Church could live with a visionary like Julian of Norwich, so long as she lived (symbolically) outside the walls of the Church, but not with a visionary like Joan of Arc, who was burned at the stake for witchcraft and heresy in 1431.

Among the common people, a popular religion had developed with the veneration of saints (particularly the Virgin Mary), relics, shrines and pilgrimages. But the vast majority of people were still excluded from participating in the central sacramental life of the Church – when they were present at Mass, they were there as spectators, excluded by and large from the Communion or Eucharist – and from any role in running Church affairs.

No longer was the Bible available in the common language, and many received their religious education only through the street plays, the carvings, paintings and stained glass in churches, or the popular cycles of folk religion. While the early primitive Church could benefit from St Jerome's translation of the Bible into the common Latin of daily commerce, the *Vulgate*, the Church in later centuries was unable to accept the demands for translation.

John Wycliffe (*c.* 1329–1384) initiated a new translation of the *Vulgate* into English, but was soon deserted by his friends in high places, and his followers, the Lollards, were suppressed. However, the demands to have the Bible translated continued apace in England and on the Continent, and the move to return to the original texts and meanings would become an essential part of the scholarship of the Renaissance.

Unlike Francis and Dominic, later critics, including the Waldensians and Hussites, were less successful in seeking to reform the Church from within. In France and Italy, the Waldensians were hunted down. In Central Europe, John Hus (1374–1415), a priest and teacher at the Charles University in Prague, stressed the authority of scripture and gave greater emphasis to preaching. He criticised with equal vigour the superstitions that had crept into popular, folk religion, the corrupt life of his clerical contemporaries, the authority assumed by cardinals and the papacy, and the withholding of the cup of wine from the people during the Communion.

At the Council of Constance in 1415, Wyclif was condemned for heresy and an order was made that his body be disinterred from holy ground; Hus too was condemned as a heretic, and without an opportunity to defend his ideas was burned at the stake. On the other hand, Thomas à Kempis (c. 1380–1471), was able to remain within the Church, and influenced many through his preaching, counselling, and books, particularly *The Imitation of Christ*, which opened the hearts and minds of many to receive the teachings of the Reformers.

The demands for reform refused to go away, and Wycliffe and Hus can be seen as precursors of the Reformation. The simple lifestyle of the Hussites and the Waldensians, who were excommunicated, or Thomas à Kempis and the Brethren of the Common Life, who remained inside the Church, provided a stark contrast to the lifestyle of many fifteenth-century popes.

The papacy had already been exposed to criticism through the political power-games of many popes in the battles between France and Germany, the lengthy absence from Rome of popes in Avignon, and the consequent schisms and the emergence of rival colleges of cardinals and claimants to the papacy. With the deposition of rival Popes in 1409, 1415 and 1417, the Councils of Pisa and Constance established an important principle: a council could deprive a pope of his claims to supremacy.

With Sixtus IV (1471–1484), the papacy reached a new low: he made six of his 'nephews' cardinals, was implicated in the assassination of two of the Medicis in 1478, and exploited the sale of offices and indulgences. Alexander VI (1492–1503), father of the infamous Lucretia Borgia, secured his election through bribery and within a year had divided the spoils of the 'New World' between Spain and Portugal. The age of discovery coincided with the Renaissance, which gave the Church great artists, including Michelangelo and Titian, and the wisdom and erudition of scholars such as Erasmus and Rabelais.

Desiderius Erasmus of Rotterdam (1467–1536) has been described as 'the greatest humanist after Petrarch'. It is said that he made the Reformation inevitable, and his monastic contemporaries complained that he laid the egg which Luther hatched. Erasmus was educated by the Brethren of the Common Life in Holland, and joined the Augustinians in 1487. In Paris, Erasmus was strongly critical of the of the nominalist theology at the Sorbonne; in Rome, he was contemptuous of the climate of corruption. Instead, he turned to the classics and the humanists, became the 'journalist of scholarship', edited Jerome's works, and in 1516 published the first printed edition of the Greek New Testament.

His friend Francois Rabelais (1494–1553) mocked the failings of the theology of the Sorbonne and was open to the ideas of the Reformers. But, while satirising the failings of Rome and the Papacy, he remained a priest throughout his life. And yet the Renaissance and the Reformation are inseparable.

After Erasmus and Rabelais, theology could never be the same again. No longer could there be an unquestioning acceptance of received tradition and teachings. The decay in the Church had produced the demands for reform, and the Renaissance provided the intellectual methods for those demanding reform.

A year after Erasmus published his Greek New Testament, the Reformation began on 31 October 1517, when the

Professor of Biblical Studies at Wittenberg University nailed his *95 Theses* to the door of the Castle Church. Decay and decline left the Church too weak to accept or meet the demands for reform.

The reformers had to be dealt with brutally – as the Dominican prior Savonarola had been burned at the stake in Florence – or marginalised and cut off by excommunication. But the demands for reform were coming from within the Church, and those leading the demands were among its most able and loyal clergy: an Augustinian friar in Germany, Martin Luther (1483–1546); a French parish priest, John Calvin (1509–1564); a French Dominican, Martin Bucer (1491–1551), who tried to mediate between Calvin and Luther; and their English contemporary, Thomas Cranmer (1489–1556), a quiet and reluctant scholar from Cambridge who was summoned to become Archbishop of Canterbury as late as 1532, and who would shape the English language through the *Book of Common Prayer* and his translation of the Psalms.

When it came, the Reformation ought to have been a breath of fresh air through the whole Church. Instead, it threatened to bring down the whole edifice.

SPIRIT OF REFORM SWEPT THROUGH THE CHURCH

The pioneer of the Reformation, Martin Luther, became an Augustinian friar in 1505 after taking a dramatic vow during a thunderstorm. He was ordained two years later, and at the age of twenty-nine became Professor of Biblical Studies at the new University of Wittenberg, where he began to challenge tradition and to emphasise personal understanding and experience of God's Word. At first, his views attracted little attention, but his career took a dramatic turn after posting his *95 Theses* to the north door of the Castle Church in Wittenberg on 31 October 1517.

The *95 Theses* were not so much a revolutionary call to reform as a young academic theologian's earnest proposals to discuss the trade in indulgences and the errors and abuses that had developed over the centuries. Luther attacked the Church's material preoccupations and contrasted the treasures of the Church with its true wealth, the Gospel.

He was censured by the Archbishop of Mainz, disputed with the Papal authorities in Augsburg and in Heidelberg, refused to recant or accept a summons to Rome, and finally was excommunicated by the Pope in 1521 and outlawed at the Diet of Worms a few months later. But he continued to write and publish, translated the Bible into German, found support among many of the princes and fired the imagination of Europe.

Theologically, Luther today appears surprisingly conservative and Catholic in many of his writings. Politically, he was dependent on his princely supporters, and when he condemned the 'murderous hordes' during the Peasants' Revolt (1524–1525), he alienated many of the ordinary people. But before long, Luther's teachings had spread widely throughout Germany, and into Eastern Europe and Scandinavia, and were influencing those waiting for an opportunity to propose reform in England.

To the south, in Zürich, Huldreich Zwingli (1484–1531), the parish priest of the Great Cathedral (Grossmünster), began to preach reform at the same time as Luther. Both had been influenced by Erasmus, but Zwingli arrived at his position independently. He had been trained in the Thomist principles, and in the steps of Aquinas he became an important systematic theologian. Zwingli was secretly married in 1522, but even as late as 1523 he received a warm letter from the Pope.

Zwingli and Luther reached deadlock in their debate over the Eucharist at Marburg in 1529, and the Swiss Reform movement lost the support of the German princes. Before long there were two main streams in the new Protest movement – the followers of Luther and the Reformed or Swiss Protestants. Zwingli met an early death on the battlefield, and his place as the leading Reformed theologian was taken by the French humanist scholar, John Calvin, who had been forced into exile from Paris, eventually settling in Geneva.

At first, Luther, Zwingli and Calvin wished to reform Church practices and teachings from within; they had no intention of leaving the Church to form new Churches, nor did they wish to break the links between Church and State and they retained the ideal of a State Church to which all citizens belonged. Luther depended on the princes for support, while Calvin had tight control over the town council in Geneva, where he tried to bring every citizen under the moral discipline of the Church, and sanctioned the arrest of the heretic Michael Servetus, who was burnt to death.

The unity of Church and State was maintained in England when the Reformation took hold only when Henry VIII – honoured by the Pope as 'Defender of the Faith' for his attack on Luther in 1521 – became entangled in a dispute with Rome after failing to receive Papal sanction for his planned divorce. The excommunicated Henry remained a Catholic in doctrine and practice until his death, and it was only during the reign of his son Edward VI (1537–1553) that the Reformation was effectively introduced. The English Reformers, led by Archbishop Thomas Cranmer of Canterbury, Bishop Nicholas Ridley (c. 1500–1555) and Bishop Hugh Latimer (c. 1485–1555), fused Lutheranism and Calvinism in a State Church that retained Catholic order and much of Catholic liturgy.

Lutheranism, the Reformed or Calvinist movement, and Anglicanism formed the three main schools of thought to arise during the Reformation. But there were more radical movements, seeking thorough-going reforms, whose members rejected state-Church links and challenged many of the traditions the principal reformers had accepted. They often rejected infant baptism and advocated radical political reform too. From these movements would arise the Baptists, Anabaptists, Mennonites and Quakers of later generations.

The Reformation may have caught Rome largely unprepared, but this situation did not continue for long. The Council of Trent, called by Pope Paul III, met in three sessions between 1545 and 1563 to redefine doctrine and to introduce sweeping reforms. Trent too must be seen as part of the great movement in the sixteenth century to reform the Church.

The Jesuits are often regarded as spearheading the Counter-Reformation attack on the Reformation, but the Society of Jesus was not founded by Ignatius Loyola (1491–1556) with the specific intention of combatting Protestants and Reform: the spirit of Reform was sweeping through Europe, including those branches of the Church that retained their links with Rome.

The heritage of medieval spirituality was found to be alive in the challenging writings of the great Spanish Carmelite mystics, Teresa of Avila (1515–1582) and her confessor, John of the Cross (1542–1591), and a new sense of mission was recovered for the whole Church by the Jesuits through the labours of Francis Xavier (1506–1552), who reached India, and Matteo Ricci (15521610) in China. Soon there were Jesuit, Franciscan, Dominican and Augustinian missionaries throughout the Americas, in the Philippines and parts of Africa.

As Europe went to war over religious differences, it may have appeared that the Reformation that first divided the Church was also sounding its death knell. Instead, the spirit of Reform swept through all branches of the Church, and within a century, all sections of the Church were finding new riches of spiritual life and a new zeal for expansion and mission.

Why didn't the Reformation take hold in Ireland?
As in England, the Tudor Reformation was an act of state in Ireland, implemented by parliamentary legislation. The Reformation was accepted by most of the bishops in 1536 when Papal supremacy was replaced by the supremacy of the State. However, the bishops made no changes in doctrine, and many of the first Reforming bishops are counted in the diocesan lists of both the Catholic Church and the Church of Ireland. The names of the early Reformers show they were drawn from the mainstream of Irish life – names such as Browne, Butler, Cullen, Devereux, Nugent, Purcell or Walsh – and the episcopal succession continued uninterrupted.

During the reign of Edward VI (1537–1553), a reformed liturgy was introduced from England and the *Book of Common Prayer*, first used in Christ Church Cathedral, Dublin, on Easter Day 1551, was the first book printed in Ireland. Under Mary (1553–1558), some Reforming bishops were deposed and married clergy punished, but the Reformation returned under Elizabeth (1558–1603), and was accepted by all but two of the bishops. In 1560, the Irish Parliament again repudiated the authority of the Pope and passed the Act of Uniformity, making Anglicanism the state religion in Ireland.

The dividing line, however, between who was Protestant and who was Catholic, was not clearly defined even a generation after the Reformation was first introduced. The case of the pluralist Miler Magrath is infamous: he managed to remain Roman Catholic Bishop of Down and Connor while he was the Church of Ireland Archbishop of Cashel. A more interesting, if less dramatic, example of the confused identities of the day is provided by Magrath's predecessor as Bishop of Achonry. Eugene O'Harte, the Dominican Prior of Sligo, who was appointed Bishop of Achonry on 28 January 1563 by Pope Pius IV. O'Harte attended the final session of the Council of

Trent, but when he returned to the west of Ireland, he was accepted as the bishop of his diocese by old Catholics and new Anglicans alike, and remained in office until he died in his hundreth year in 1603.

Historians continue to debate why the Reformation never took hold at a popular level in Ireland. The Church historian Canon Michael Burrowes points out in his study of the episcopacy in Ireland: 'The reasons why the bulk of the Irish population did not . . . adopt Protestantism, but rather came to look to Rome for alternative structures and pastoral care, remain hotly contested'.

SOWING THE SEEDS OF CULTURAL REVIVAL

The divisions the Reformation brought to the Church in western and northern Europe in the sixteenth and early seventeenth century failed to bring an end to many of the problems the Reformers first hoped to end. Theological differences often gave an excuse for political divisions, giving them an expression that allowed warring factions and those engaged in civil commotion to invoke God's name, and to fight on believing or claiming to have right on their side. From 1618 to 1648, the Thirty Years War was a continuous series of conflicts between Catholic and Protestant princes, involving France, Sweden and the German states of the declining Empire. The political rivalry between England and France only served to deepen the religious divisions in Scotland.

In England, the suppression of more radical reformers led to the emigration of many Puritans in the early seventeenth century to new colonies, where the Pilgrim Fathers and others sowed the seeds for change and revolution in North America in later generations. Those Puritans who stayed behind would pave the way for the rise of Cromwell, and, in a distant but direct way, would also pave the way for the rise of parliamentary democracy in Britain.

Cromwell's Commonwealth gave new energy to the more radical post-Reformation movements, including Baptists and Congregationalists, and to new movements such as the Quakers. Had it not been so short-lived, Cromwell's rule might have brought an end to episcopacy in England, destroyed the Anglican Reformation and allowed the rise, growth and multiplication of many more sects, bringing further, deeper divisions within Christianity. But episcopacy survived in the Church of Ireland, and Irish bishops played a key role in putting the Church of England on a new foundation after the restoration of Charles II. It was an exchange that proved to be mutually beneficial: one of the great English theologians of the period was Jeremy Taylor who came to Ireland as Bishop of Down, Connor and Dromore, while the earliest Anglican hymn writers include the Irish poets Nahum Tate, poet laureate, and Nicholas Brady, chaplain to William and Mary.

The seventeenth century also demonstrated a new spirit of intellectual inquiry, however, characterised in France and the Netherlands by René Descartes, who sought proof for the existence of God, and summarised his philosophy in the dictum *Cogito ergo sum* ('I think, therefore I am'), the mathematician and philosopher, Blaise Pascal, and by Cornelius Otto Jansen and the Jansenists, condemned posthumously by Pope Innocent X.

The seventeenth century was also one of monumental building – Saint Peter's was completed in Rome in 1656, Christopher Wren began work on Saint Paul's Cathedral in London in 1675, and the Counter-Reformation found 'its ultimate expression' in the Baroque architecture of Italy and Spain, which soon spread to Austria, southern Germany and France.

It was a century of monumental art – Protestantism found its supreme expression in painting, particularly in the Dutch school, exemplified by Rembrandt and his biblical subjects. It was also a century of monumental writing – John Donne had been Dean of Saint Paul's, John Milton's *Paradise Lost* dates from 1665 and John Bunyan's *Pilgrim's Progress* was published in 1678. It was, however, a century of persecution and suppression too. Bunyan had been jailed in Bedford in 1660, the Huguenots lost their religious liberty in France with the Revocation of the Edict of Nantes in 1685, and Louis XIV struck out against the Jansenists, destroying their spiritual centre at Port Royal.

The conflicts and wars in the immediate aftermath of the Reformation appeared to have consumed the energies of the Churches, leaving them exhausted by the end of the seventeenth century, and the Church of the eighteenth century, pilloried in the cartoons of William Hogarth, was in need of revitalisation. But there were signs of renewal and vision throughout Europe. In England, the first missionary societies were formed through the energies of the Rector of Sheldon, Thomas Bray, who helped found both the Society for Promoting Christian Knowledge (SPCK) in 1698 and the Society for the Propagation of the Gospel (SPG, now USPG) in 1701, whose early missionaries in North America included George Berkeley.

The way was being prepared for a new cultural, intellectual and spiritual awakening throughout the Christian world. In Germany, Philip Jacob Spenner, author of *Pia Desideria*, gave rise to Lutheran Pietism before his death in 1705. Soon, Johann Sebastian Bach was at work, inscribing the scores of his religious work at the beginning with the letters 'JJ' (*Jesu juva*, Jesus help) at the beginning, and at the end with 'SDG' (*Soli Deo Gloria*, to God alone the glory).

In Ireland and England, Handel was working on his oratorios, including Messiah. The churches were producing philosophers of the calibre of George Berkeley, Bishop of Cloyne and a former SPG missionary, and Joseph Butler, Bishop of Durham. In North America, Jonathan Edwards sparked the revival known as the Great Awakening in 1734. It had subsided four years later, but in England in 1738, John Wesley underwent a remarkable spiritual experience in London. When he died in 1791, Wesley had travelled 225,000 miles on horseback, preached forty thousand sermons, and left seventy thousand Methodists in Britain and Ireland, and there were sixty thousand more in America.

A spirit of renewal also took a hold on the Orthodox Churches of Eastern Europe. For three hundred years, the Ottoman occupation had weakened their inner vitality, and they were under pressure from Islam and the Enlightenment rationalists. But a spiritual revival began on Mount Athos, the monastic peninsula in northern Greece, where Bishop Nicholas Kalliboutzes (Saint Nicodemus) edited the *Philokalia* and sparked new interest in the Jesus Prayer, the prayer of the heart which spread throughout Europe: 'Lord Jesus Christ, have mercy on me, the sinner'.

The independence of theological inquiry, however, was under threat in parts of Western Europe. The Jesuits were banished from Portugal in 1759, they were expelled from France in 1764, 5,000 were deported from Spain and the Spanish empire in 1767, and the Society of Jesus was suppressed by Pope Clement XIV in 1773. Suppression of the Jansenists and Jesuits in France did not end independent thinking and inquiry, and a Church that had been intellectually disarmed could do little to reply to the criticism of Voltaire and Rousseau, and found itself unprepared for the tide of revolution. In Ireland, fear of the spread of French revolutionary ideas contributed in part to the formation of the Orange Order in 1795 and, in the same year, the foundation with government funds of the Royal College of Saint Patrick at Maynooth.

The SPCK and the SPG, founded by Bray, had at first

confined their work to the British colonies, but among the Protestant Churches, missionary work was expanding through the formation of the Baptist Missionary Society (1792), the London Missionary Society (1796), and the Church Missionary Society (1799). Christianity, threatened by the wars, revolutions, internal conflicts and philosophical questioning of the seventeenth and eighteenth centuries, was about to launch its greatest drive towards expansion and growth, and about to face its greatest intellectual challenges.

A REARGUARD ACTION AGAINST THE INDUSTRIAL REVOLUTION

The nineteenth century opened with crowning events that marked it as a century of conflict between Church and State and between religion and reason. In 1801, Napoleon signed a new concordat with Pius VII in which the State was given a veto over the appointment of bishops by the Pope and over the appointment of lower clergy by the bishops, and Protestants were granted freedom of religion. The Pope had given grudging assent to the revolution and, in 1804, Pius VII sat as a pathetic spectator while Napoleon crowned himself emperor. Four years later, Napoleon took the papal states and the Pope was soon exiled to Fontainebleau, near Paris.

The experiences were humiliating for the papacy and shook the Church to its core. In France, in previous centuries, Gallicanism had challenged the power of the popes. In Germany and Austria, there were new challenges from those who argued that the Pope was in fact only the first among equals, and the primary source of authority was Church councils. Once the papacy returned to the Vatican, the Jesuits were reorganised and a new movement, Ultramontanism ('beyond the mountains') arose to promote the supreme authority of the Pope in matters of faith and practice. The Catholic Church, however, continued to face assault from liberal and republican political thought. Pope Gregory XVI and Pope Pius IX fought liberalism and the moves to unite Italy. As a new revolutionary fervour swept France, Italy and Germany, Mazzini and Garibaldi succeeded in forcing Pius IX into exile in 1848. When he returned to Rome two years later, his earlier liberal sympathies had vanished.

As political power ebbed away from Pius, he put increasing emphasis on his spiritual powers. He re-established the Catholic hierarchies in England and the Netherlands, and signed concordats with Russia, Spain and Austria. In 1854, he proclaimed the doctrine of Mary's Immaculate Conception. In 1864, he issued the *Syllabus of Errors* in which political liberalism was condemned, along with rationalism, liberal theology, religious toleration, the Bible Societies, civil marriages and freemasonry. And in 1869, he summoned the first Vatican Council.

The council had an in-built majority in favour of the Ultramontanists – 279 Italian bishops and 265 bishops from all other European states – and it strengthened his power inside the church by proclaiming papal infallibility on July 13th, 1870.

The Ultramontanists had triumphed over Gallicanism and the liberal bishops. Pius rebuked one dissenting bishop with the words: 'Tradition; I am tradition.' The German Church historian Döllinger refused to be silenced and was excommunicated. Yet the Pope's political strength had been irreversibly weakened; in 1870 the city of Rome was incorporated in the new united Italy, leaving the Pope with only the Vatican, the Lateran and Castel Gandolfo from the former papal states.

In France, Napoleon III was forced to choose between Catholicism and the national interest, and chose the latter. In Germany, the Prussian chancellor, Bismarck, initiated the *Kulturkampf* against the Catholic Church and seriously weakened the legal status of Catholics, leading to the expulsion of the Jesuits and the state taking control of education.

Leo XIII had a calming influence on Church-State relations in Germany and in France, where he urged Catholics to abandon royalism and accept the republic. In his encyclical *Rerum Novarum* (1891), he pleaded for social reform and for trade unionism to ensure workers received a proper wage. The papacy had woken up to the threats and promises of the industrial revolution.

Since its dawning in the 1760s, the industrial revolution was challenging morals and values. While some evangelicals found common cause with the new morality of industrial capitalism, others could see the dismal lot of those who laboured in William Blake's 'dark satanic mills' and Charles Dickens' Coketown, with its 'interminable serpents of smoke'. The repeal of the Test and Corporation Acts in 1828 and Catholic emancipation in 1829 had given some Catholics and nonconformists in Britain and Ireland the right to vote and to sit in parliament, but the rights and plight of the working class, Catholic or Protestant, had still to be addressed.

At first, the parish system of the Church of England was unable to respond to the industrial revolution and the needs of the new urban masses it had thrown up. But the evangelicalism that had moved William Wilberforce, Fowell Buxton and the 'Clapham Sect' to labour for the abolition of the slave trade in 1807 and of slavery in 1833 was the same evangelicalism that, a generation later, worked to ease the hard lot of factory workers.

Christian socialism first emerged in the writings of Charles Kingsley, better remembered today for *The Water Babies* and *Westward Ho!*, and F. D. Maurice. It is often pointed out that the Tolpuddle Martyrs were firm Christians and it is frequently repeated that the Labour Party in Britain owed more to Methodism than Marxism. Faced with the challenges of Charles

Darwin and Karl Marx, however, the Church often retreated into itself to address only its own agenda.

The Oxford Movement – led by John Keble, John Henry Newman, Edward Pusey and Henry Manning – was brought together first by their concern at legislative measures aimed at the Church of Ireland. It inspired the great hymns of Newman and Lyte, the architecture of Pugin, the poetry of the Rossettis, the paintings of the pre-Raphaelites and many in the arts and crafts movement. As a movement, however, it often appeared more concerned with Church order, sacramental life, Church architecture and liturgy than with mission and the state of the world. Newman, Manning, Pugin and many others drifted to Rome and it was another generation before Bishop Charles Gore and the essayists who contributed to *Lux Mundi* found a vibrant combination of theology, mission and politics. Their circle included the Cambridge New Testament scholar and future Bishop of Durham, Brooke Foss Westcott, first president of the Christian Social Union and one of the early pioneers of historic and literary criticism and of modern theology.

An inward-looking Pietism sometimes broke its bonds: the new movements of the nineteenth century included the Dublin-born Plymouth Brethren, who typified the temptation to withdraw from the world, but also included the YMCA, founded by George Williams, and the Salvation Army, founded by William Booth.

European continental theology had been enriched in the nineteenth century by Immanuel Kant, Friedrich Schleiermacher and Søren Kierkegaard. Missionary work saw its frontiers expanded through the labours of men such as David Livingstone. The Church in America, however, was deeply divided by the issue of slavery, while the Church in Europe, forced into retreat by the challenges of the industrial revolution and the writings of Darwin and Marx, was weakened by the defensiveness of Pius IX and the inward-looking Pietism that threatened to dominate Protestantism. Was Christianity prepared to face the challenges of the twentieth century?

On Christianity's margins
The nineteenth century saw the growth of a number of new movements. The Plymouth Brethren trace themselves back to an evangelical revival on the Powerscourt estate in County Wicklow and the early preachings of John Nelson Darby, a former Church of Ireland clergyman.

The Seventh Day Adventists were founded by William Miller, who announced that the Second Coming of Christ would take place in 1843, or at the latest by October 1844.

Today, the Plymouth Brethren are generally accepted as part of mainstream evangelical Christianity, although they often remain marginalised. However, other groups that arose in the nineteenth century put themselves beyond the margins of the Christian tradition with their additional beliefs and books.

The Church of Jesus Christ of Latter Day Saints was founded by Joseph Smith, who claimed he had translated the *Book of Mormon* in 1844. The movement settled in Salt Lake City in 1847, and is commonly known today as The Mormons.

The Christian Scientists, or the Church of Christ Scientist, was founded in 1879 by Mary Baker Eddy, with a system of beliefs based on her book *Science and Health with a Key to the Scriptures*. Later marginal groups would include the Jehovah's Witnesses.

CHURCH CONFRONTING A CENTURY OF CHANGE
In the twentieth-century the experiences of two world wars, the devastation that was the Holocaust, the shadow of the atomic cloud over Hiroshima, and the end of colonialism shaped both

theology and moves towards ecumenism where all Churches were concerned.

Perhaps its most influential theologian was the Swiss-born Karl Barth (1886–1968). A product of the great liberal schools of theology developed in the nineteenth-century German-speaking world, Barth was influenced at an early age by his readings of Kierkegaard and Dostoevsky. He trained at Bern, Berlin, Tübingen and Marburg, but none of these prepared him for his experiences as a war-time chaplain. The horrors of the First World War forced him to challenge the dominant assumptions of liberal theology and the close links between Church and State, which are cemented during any major war.

His first book, a commentary on *The Epistle to the Romans* (1919), 'landed like a bombshell in the playground of the theologians'. His *Church Dogmatics* (1932) is without parallel in length and thoroughness, dwarfing even Thomas Aquinas' *Summa Theologica*. With the rise of the Nazis, Barth and Martin Niemöller formed the Pastors' Emergency League, which later became the Confessing Church. In 1934 they adopted the Barmen Declaration, which challenged pro-Nazi elements in the Churches, but also became one of the seminal documents of twentieth-century theology.

Heroes of the resistance included a young pastor from a secular family, Dietrich Bonhöffer, who was hanged in April 1945. His best-known pre-war book, *The Cost of Discipleship*, made the distinction between 'cheap grace' and 'costly grace', and along with his *Letters and Papers from Prison* and *Ethics* had a profound influence on post-war theology.

At the same time in America, Bonhöffer's friend, Reinhold Niebuhr (1892–1971) of Detroit, was drawing attention to the injustices of capitalism in a modern, technical society. Rejecting liberal optimism also, he developed the concepts of social and historical sin. In England, Archbishop William Temple expressed the need for social and economic justice in any post-war society.

In the Vatican, however, modernism and liberalism, and later communism, were seen as the greatest threats facing the world. Although papal encyclicals in 1937 condemned both Nazism and communism, Pope Pius XII would be accused of not having done enough to resist the evils of fascism and Nazism, and of not speaking out loud enough against the Holocaust.

Post-war theology was shaped by the evil of the Holocaust and the potential for nuclear annihilation. Jews such as Martin Buber and Elie Wiesel would influence future generations of theologians and liberal theology found it hard to regain ground.

The international ecumenical movement traces its origins to the Edinburgh Missionary Conference of 1910. This initiative was interrupted by the First World War, but the impetus from Edinburgh led to the formation of two movements: 'Life and Work' in 1925 and 'Faith and Order' in 1927. These merged after the Second World War into the World Council of Churches, formed at Amsterdam in 1948.

The declaration of the Assumption of Mary as an infallible dogma by Pius XII in 1950 seemed to point to a Catholic Church not yet open to ecumenical developments. Then Pope John XXIII called the Second Vatican Council and the world was surprised by its ecumenical focus. Tridentine Catholicism came to an end, liturgical reform was sweeping, and doors to dialogue opened. Decolonisation hastened self-government and indigenousness in the Churches. It inspired renewed ecumenical moves, with the formation of united Churches in northern and southern India, Pakistan and Bangladesh. In the West, the Congregational Church and the Presbyterian Church in England joined in 1972 to form the United Reformed Church.

Although the Church of England and the Methodists failed to unite despite numerous attempts, and the Vatican appeared to reject various reports of the Anglican-Roman Catholic International Commissions (ARCIC), the Anglican and Lutheran Churches came closer to forming one communion with the Meissen and Porvoo agreements. Recently, the US Episcopal and Lutheran Churches united.

In the 1960s, Billy Graham became the most recognised evangelical preacher, while Pentecostal and Charismatic movements grew rapidly. There was also a renewed interest in liberal theology. In 1963 John Robinson's *Honest to God* was a bestseller, while the 'God is Dead' controversy made the front cover of Time magazine.

The civil rights movement in the US was led by a black Baptist pastor from Alabama, the Rev. Martin Luther King. In Europe, issues such as environment and nuclear disarmament came to the fore, with Canon John Collins leading the first generation of the Campaign for Nuclear Disarmament. Monsignor Bruce Kent and Canon Paul Oestreicher were to the fore in a second generation. In America, the Jesuit Berrigan brothers were among the leaders of Vietnam War protests.

There was an explosive growth of churches in Africa, Asia and Latin America. In Latin America, liberation theology was boosted by the meeting of Latin American bishops in Medellin in 1968. Its principal proponent was Gustavo Gutierrez, author of *A Theology of Liberation* (1971). Hans Küng's *On being a Christian* (1974) proved that theology could sell.

By the 1980s and 1990s, it would have been easy to accuse European and North American Churches of being more concerned with internal agendas – liturgical reform, the ordination of women, or the disciplining of prophetic theologians such as Hans Küng, Leonardo Boff and Lavinia Byrne. But there were also signs of an outward-looking Church in agencies such as Christian Aid, Cafod and Trócaire. Nuclear pacifism had become the accepted Christian stand on war in the nuclear age – expressed in Archbishop Robert Runcie's controversial sermon at the Falklands memorial service, which angered Margaret Thatcher.

Pax Christi and the Fellowship of Reconciliation flourished alongside the ministries of the Corrymeela Centre, Coventry Cathedral, and George McLeod's Iona Community. In East Germany and Poland, the Churches were catalysts in the fall of communism. In South Africa they played a crucial role in bringing down apartheid, symbolised in Bishop Desmond Tutu receiving the Nobel Peace Prize.

Reaction and retrenchment in the Vatican under Pope John Paul II and Cardinal Joseph Ratzinger, symbolised in the efforts to ban the use of the term 'sister Churches', caused many to wonder whether the Churches were entering an ecumenical winter.

Despite this, the enduring memories of late twentieth-century Christianity may well be the vivid images of Pope John Paul and Archbishop Robert Runcie kneeling together in prayer at Canterbury Cathedral.

Movers and shakers
The twentieth century has produced outstanding theologians, including Karl Barth, Albert Schweizer, Rudolf Bultmann, Oscar Culmann, Reinhold Niebuhr, Emil Brunner, Dietrich Bonhöffer, Pierre Teilhard de Chardin, Paul Tillich, Wolfhart Pannenberg, Karl Rahner, Hans Küng, Edward Schillebeeckx and Jurgen Moltmann, as well as the writers of Liberation Theology in Latin America, and indigenous theologians such as Kosuke Koyama in Japan and John Mbiti in Kenya. But theology also received critical input from writers, artists and architects such as T. S. Eliot, C. S. Lewis, Evelyn Underhill, Graham Sutherland and Basil Spence.

In many ways, Canon Paul Oestreicher is one man who embodies the Church of the twentieth century and its struggles. Born into a Jewish family in Germany, he fled to New Zealand at the age of seven in 1938. As a schoolboy, he became a Christian and later he was ordained a priest in the Church of England. A founding figure in Amnesty International, he also campaigned against the nuclear arms race and apartheid. He was an early pioneer of Christian-Marxist dialogue and was a keen supporter of the ordination of women. Committed to ecumenism, he became a Quaker with the permission of his bishop while still an Anglican priest.

Canon Oestreicher's perceived radical politics led to his election as a bishop in New Zealand being blocked. His final years in ministry before retirement were spent as a canon in Coventry Cathedral – perhaps the one building that has had the most influence on twentieth-century Church architecture and art; it also symbolised post-war reconciliation. There he was in charge of the Cathedral's 'Cross of Nails' ministry of reconciliation until his retirement two years ago. Last year, at the height of the Balkans war, he travelled to Belgrade.

TAKING A RUNNING JUMP AT THE FUTURE

We have been looking at the history of Christianity and the Church during the last two thousand years. No religious tradition that gives a special place to historical documents and tests its rituals and practices against the experiences, teachings and customs of the past can ignore the lessons of history, but any exercise in history can be compared to a child taking a few steps back so she can have a good run and leap out into the future.

Over the centuries, the same debates have surfaced time and again in the Church: the nature of the relationship between God and Jesus Christ; the conflict between charism and institution; the competing or complementary claims of defining salvation through faith expressed in assent or through faith expressed in practice; the rift between the Greek East and the Latin West; the boundaries between political power and the community of faith; an understanding of mission as conversion or proselytism or as witness and presence; the efforts to refine and purify the Church and the competing demand to maintain Church unity. On the other hand, many of the divisions of the past now seem to have been laid to rest.

The divisions between East and West may prove to be more difficult, however, and even the Orthodox, according to Sergei Hackel, accept that their own fissile divisions 'make us poor potential neighbours should we persist in trying to be neighbours at all.' But last year's agreement between Lutherans and Roman Catholics on 'justification by faith alone' laid to rest 450 years of division, and there is an argument that all continuing divisions between the Churches are based more on pride and tribal loyalty than on any continuing major doctrinal differences.

At the same time, the Church needs to be reminded of the lessons from past debates and the value of the doctrinal formulations they produced. Dr Maurice Wiles, former Regius Professor of Divinity at Oxford, recently recalled showing another leading liberal theologian the slogan: 'Not back to the creeds but forward from the creeds.' His colleague commented: 'That's rather a good statement of what's needed.' Only then did he disclose that the slogan was used by the pro-Nazi German Christians as they were seizing control of the German churches. In the mid-twentieth century, Karl Barth and Dietrich Bonhöffer provided a stark warning of the dangers of theology drifting too close to the cultural and political fashions of the day.

We might ask what is the future for theology? The past generation has seen the growth of more specific and more actively committed forms of theology, such as liberation theology, feminist theology, political theology, black theology and indigenous theologies. And a significant development in recent years is what Dr Wiles describes as 'confessional approaches to theology' that stand in the general tradition of Barth. These place a new emphasis on Scripture, the traditional Christian beliefs, particularly the doctrine of the Trinity, and often with concern for wider implications for society and issues such as the environment. But none of these schools necessarily holds the only option for theology in the coming century; as Dr Wiles warns, 'every attempt to speak sensibly and appropriately about God and God's relation to the world is bound to be partial and provisional, in need of correction.'

We may no longer see the days when theological books are best sellers and stir public controversy as did John Robinson's *Honest to God* in the 1960s, Hans Küng's *On Being a Christian*, or the *Myth of God Incarnate*, edited by John Hick, in the 1970s. But Christianity will continue to influence and shape culture, as it did in the past with Michelangelo's frescoes and sculptures, Mozart's Requiems and Masses, and in paintings, poetry, drama and architecture. Even today's language of management and business has adapted the language of faith and theology in 'mission statements' or terms such as 'urban regeneration'.

The Church itself is aware of its own need for a fresh commitment to mission and regeneration. But who can predict the future shape of the Church? In the 1970s, Charismatics claimed they held the future of the Church in their hands. At the beginning of the twenty-first century, many evangelicals are prepared to make this claim. But there are swings and pendulums, and theology and approaches to spirituality are also victims of fashion.

Today, differences and agreements in theology cut across denominational boundaries. Although we may be in an ecumenical winter and documents such as *Dominus Iesus* have dealt a severe blow to ecumenism, it is certain that the future of theology and the future of the Church is ecumenical.

Kathleen Norris, in her highly acclaimed recent book, *The Cloister Walk*, has pointed out yet again how women are written out when it comes to writing the history of the Church. And it is beyond doubt that women will gain their rightful place in the Church in the near future.

Perhaps one of the major unresolved questions at the beginning of this new century is the depth of any future relationship with the other two principal monotheistic faiths, Judaism and Islam. There is no doubt that there must be dialogue and that centuries of unresolved, unnecessary and sinful conflict must end. But the degree of mutual coexistence in some societies has to be debated before even talking about shared social action or even the theological bases for exploring shared worship.

In his book, *The Death of Christian Britain*, Dr Callum Brown of Strathclyde University argues that within a generation Christianity will be a minority cult in Britain, and he predicts the same fate for the whole of Western Christianity. But whether one predicts an exciting future for Christianity or its decline and demise depends not just on skills in long-term weather forecasting, but on basic theological and faith assumptions. Even if a Christian accepted the forecasts of the decline of Christianity, faith assumes a continuing Christian presence in the world.

Mission is not about business models of meeting growth targets or increasing donors and donations, but on making the Christian message present and effective in the world, and, as the Anglican Consultative Council defined mission, also includes responding 'to human need by service', seeking 'to transform unjust structures of society', and striving to 'safeguard the integrity of creation and sustain and renew the earth'.

Professor Wiles, in a recent paper in the journal *Theology*, recalls a BBC producer expressing amazement on learning that he would be preaching in a village church on Christmas morning. 'It was a matter of surprise to him that a theologian of my ilk should be preaching at all, let alone on Christmas Day of all days.' But the first place for theologians is in the pulpit and with the community of faith on Christmas Day, Easter Day, and Sunday by Sunday. After that, all theology and all Church history is merely explication and explanation.